A T I O N A L B E S T S E L L E R

PRAISE FOR HAYLEY WICKENHEISER

"An enjoyable and memorable read for all hockey fans, whether you're more interested in the nitty-gritty details of Wickenheiser's four Olympic gold medal runs or the opportunity for self-improvement." —IIHF.com

"I have looked up to Hayley Wickenheiser as someone who has been inspiring Canadians on and off the ice for many years. In *Over the Boards*, Hayley gives you a peek into the lessons and philosophies that helped make her the leader she is. From insights and advice on competing each day, leading from the heart, and, of course, leaving a legacy, you will find yourself equipped to take on whatever challenges lay ahead." —**Harnarayan Singh,** *Hockey Night in Canada* **commentator and bestselling author of** *One Game at a Time*

"*Over the Boards* is an absolute must-read sports memoir." —*Daily Hive*

"Hayley—now Doctor—Wickenheiser shares grit and determination, along with anecdotes you won't see on TSN or Sportsnet, in her fabulous new book *Over the Boards: Lessons from the Ice*. This page-turning offering from someone who knows how to win at the highest level and how to take loss as a great opportunity to grow and improve is for everyone. Read and learn how #22 continues to do it all—and do it well. There are so many elements of this champion's methods you can add to your own life." —**Clara Hughes, O.C., O.M., 6x Olympic medalist, bestselling author of** *Open Heart, Open Mind*

"*Over the Boards*: Wickenheiser reminds us that we have the power to do more and to become more in our lives." —**Karl Subban, bestselling author of** *How We Did It*

"Hayley Wickenheiser is an incredible human being . . . this is what a billion hours of hard work looks like." —**Ryan Reynolds**

"A detailed and rare look at greatness—one of Canada's most decorated athletes pulls back the veil on what propelled her to the top. Hayley Wickenheiser has written the playbook of all playbooks. *Over the Boards: Lessons from the Ice* is for anyone who wants to win in any industry from business to science to sports to the arts. But what makes this book a gem is how it prepares you for success in the most important and formidable arena of all: life." **—Perdita Felicien, Olympian and bestselling author of *My Mother's Daughter***

"Hayley is a world-class athlete with a world-class mind, and leadership skills to match. And now she's an MD. When she has something to say, people should listen." **—Brian Burke, president of hockey operations of the Pittsburgh Penguins and bestselling author of *Burke's Law***

OVER THE BOARDS

LESSONS FROM THE ICE

Hayley Wickenheiser

PENGUIN

an imprint of Penguin Canada,
a division of Penguin Random House Canada Limited

First published in Viking Canada hardcover, 2021

Published in this edition, 2022

1 2 3 4 5 6 7 8 9 10

Distributed by Penguin Random House Canada Limited, Toronto.

LIBRARY AND ARCHIVES CANADA CATALOGUING IN PUBLICATION
Title: Over the boards : lessons from the ice / Hayley Wickenheiser.
Names: Wickenheiser, Hayley, 1978- author.
Description: Previously published: Viking Canada, 2021.
Identifiers: Canadiana 20200405241 | ISBN 9780735240520 (softcover)
Subjects: LCSH: Wickenheiser, Hayley, 1978- | LCSH: Women hockey players—Canada—Biography. | LCSH: Hockey players—Canada—Biography. | LCGFT: Autobiographies.
Classification: LCC GV878.5.W53 A3 2022 | DDC 796.962092—dc23

Cover and book design: Andrew Roberts
Cover image: © Dave Holland Photography

Printed in the United States of America

www.penguinrandomhouse.ca

Penguin
Random House
PENGUIN CANADA

*To my mom and dad, who taught us
that a girl can do anything that a boy can do*

CONTENTS

PROLOGUE

It's been a long time since I was a rookie.

When people hear my name, the first thing they think is hockey. For more than 30 years, the game was my life. What most people don't know is that I held another dream for almost as long as I was a hockey player. Since I was a kid, I dreamed of being a doctor.

Which is how, after 23 years with Team Canada and six Olympics, I found myself back as a rookie, this time in medicine.

I didn't start med school until after I had retired from playing in 2017, but my transition had been in the works since 2010. My first real exposure to what life was like for physicians came thanks to the game, actually. When I was playing, I had a tough time sleeping after games—especially if we had lost or played poorly. Instead of tossing and turning for hours, I started spending those sleepless nights shadowing one of my friends, an emergency room doctor. She let me watch quietly from the back corners of the trauma bay, silently taking it all in. Over six years, I spent hundreds of nighttime hours watching trauma teams work on patients, as I slowly chipped away at my undergrad and master's degrees and continued playing during my days.

It became clear pretty quickly that medicine was the right fit for me. I usually entered the hospital preoccupied but always left the ER feeling light and happy. It sounds strange—that spending hours watching horrible injuries and medical emergencies being treated would have a calming or uplifting effect on me—but what I observed in hospital gave me perspective on the world beyond hockey. No injury, pressure-filled game, or conflict I ever went through on Team Canada was remotely comparable to the awful tragedies I witnessed in the ER. It was a huge reality check: all the day-to-day problems that had taken up residence in my mind no longer felt so huge. And all those hours watching medical staff help people made me excited for what my life could hold after my retirement from the game.

My first day as a med student dawned bright and sunny—a perfect, late summer day. The doctor I'd been shadowing invited me to spend a few hours with her in the ER. She wanted to celebrate my entrance to med school. I'd finally made it. This time, I wouldn't be shadowing. Now that I'd been admitted, being an official med student meant that I held insurance and could assist in treating patients under the supervision of a licensed physician. I'd already had some basic first aid training and was CPR certified. It was hard to believe that my dream, so long in the making, was finally coming true. I was excited. I was also anxious about what was coming down the pike: the exams, the stress, the unknown.

Because I'd spent so much time in the ER already, I felt fairly confident going in as a medical student for the first time. All my exposure to the trauma room had familiarized me with hospital codes, doctor shorthand, and medical lingo. I'd watched teams leap into action over and over. I was comfortable with the pace. Or so I thought.

A few minutes into the shift, we received a call that a patient was on their way. It was a suspected drug overdose. Firefighters had been working on a young man for 30 minutes already. They weren't sure how long he had been down before they arrived.

My supervising physician turned to me: "You are performing CPR." No easing me in; I'd be jumping headfirst into this hands-on experience. "Gown, gloves, mask on. He will be here in five minutes—let's go!"

I panicked.

My heart rate spiked. I started breathing fast. I lost my bearings—it took a few seconds to remember where the protective gear was kept. I fumbled getting my gown on. Everything and everyone around me were moving so fast—those hours I had put in shadowing doctors, all those nights I had spent watching from the sidelines: it felt like all that experience had disappeared. In that moment, when I was about to perform CPR on a patient for the first time, when it meant helping to save someone, panic superseded what my brain knew. It took over. I had watched all this stuff happen and now, on my first shift actually helping, all I could think was *I'm not qualified. What am I doing here?*

That's the thing about panic, nerves, anxiety. Those emotions have the ability to push all the knowledge you have from your brain. If you let them.

The patient hadn't arrived yet. I was trying to tie back my hair and those familiar movements forged a connection in my brain. It reminded me of tying back my hair before a game.

And suddenly, everything slowed down.

It hit me that I'd handled high-pressure situations hundreds of times before. I knew how to calm my mind. I knew how to push aside the panic and anxiety and access the knowledge I had.

I took a breath and told myself, *Get a grip.*

I isolated what my specific job was—CPR. Not so difficult: all I had to do was put the heel of my hand at the centre of the patient's chest and do compressions. Others around me would perform their roles. I had to push 30 times to the tempo of "Stayin' Alive." I repeated the song over and over to myself as I pushed. At one point, my glasses fell off and got kicked into a corner. All I kept thinking was *Do your job. Just do your job.* I took solace in knowing that I was the rookie. There were 10 vets in the room with me. I could count on them to guide me through this, in the same way Danielle Goyette, Angela James, Geraldine Heaney, and France St-Louis had guided me in my first games for Team Canada when I was a teen.

For the next 40 minutes, I performed CPR in two-minute intervals, trading off with a partner. Everyone else did what they were supposed to do. I don't remember exactly what was going on around me. I was pretty focused on my job. There were fire-fighters standing off to the side, watching. A couple of nurses put in an IV and attached monitors to the young patient. Then the doctor told me to stop. It was over. She declared his time of death.

He was the same age as my son. Looking at him lying there, I could imagine what he must have looked like as a little boy. I kept thinking about his poor mom and shed a few silent tears for them both. The team had to quickly move on to get ready for the next trauma, but I stood there for a few moments, my hand on his arm, wondering what had led him to this ending.

"I hope wherever you're going is a beautiful place," I said. In that moment, he looked like he was asleep. At peace. It was tough to walk away. It hit me hard. I still think about him. We did all that we could to save him. It wasn't enough.

I faced a steep learning curve that day and in the weeks and months that followed. But I realized that, while I may be a rookie again, I already had an arsenal of skills that I could rely on in my new career. I just had to transfer them to this new playing field.

This book was born from that day in the ER. In the panic that overwhelmed me when the call came in, I realized that I'd been there before. Not in a life or death situation, but in a high-pressure one. And I knew how to handle pressure. I'd been training for it for more than two decades.

Obviously, treating a teenaged overdose victim has higher stakes than an Olympic final. When you have a human life in your hands, the decisions you make are crucial. It's a very different type and degree of pressure. But the strategies I'd honed on the ice—focus, teamwork, leadership—were just as useful in the ER.

The game of hockey has given me a lot—more than I ever gave it. It provided me a beautiful son, a purpose, a satisfying career, and lifelong friends. But more than that, my time in hockey prepared me for everything that came next, with key lessons and strategies that I use outside the parameters of the game clock. That's what these pages contain: the lessons I have learned throughout my career. When I realized that the skills I had learned in hockey were transferable to my career in medicine, I got to thinking that they could be useful for other people as well.

I've been super lucky. Early in my life, I found something that I loved to do, and I was able to earn a living doing it. Being passionate about my work has been key to my success. It gave me inspiration each day, allowing me to keep working hard, to continue pushing my game, my speed, my shot, my fitness level. It was never about the salary or even medals. I loved the training every bit as much as I did the games. I was happiest when I was sweating through a bike ride or doing sprints in the pool. I loved the pain, the burning sensation in the pit of my lungs.

Looking back, I realize I was able to achieve all that I have by applying hard work and passion to everything that I did. That's what I really want to convey with this book. You don't have to be born with innate talent or skill—that will only take you so far. What you need to achieve your own best, the passion and perseverance, is already inside you.

There was one other reason I wanted to put pen to paper. Being female in male-dominated fields like hockey and medicine isn't easy. I want anyone who has been judged as less capable because of their gender to know that I've waded through the same bullshit as them. If my words make things a little bit easier for them or help them see that if I can do it, they can, too, it will have been worth it. We all need a little inspiration from time to time.

A lot of these lessons I learned the hard way. Take advantage of my mistakes, please! Learn from them so you can go out and make new ones. This book isn't just for athletes or medical professionals. We're all juggling multiple roles. We get swept up by heady expectations. We feel weighed down by our packed schedules. These lessons helped me get where I am and get through the challenges I've faced. I hope you can use them to help you achieve your own dreams.

Old habits die hard (which is why you have to build good ones—you'll get to that chapter), and it made the most sense to me to organize these lessons into three zones, like the game of hockey. You won't get far without a solid foundation and trusted systems, which is what the defensive zone covers; the neutral zone leans more towards learning to get comfortable being uncomfortable; and the offensive zone is where you capitalize, where you let fly and score. That's how I think about the lessons and my life, anyway. This book covers everything from when I was trying to claw my way to the top to the day I hung up my skates. A few lessons I learned off the ice have snuck in as well.

What you're not going to find in these pages are tired clichés about following your dreams. I'm a very practical person, and I like tangible ideas that can be executed. A lot of people beat around the bush. I'm a straight shooter. I don't sugar-coat things. I think it's important to be direct and say what you mean.

And for better or for worse, I always have.

THE DEFENSIVE ZONE

Build your foundation

I HAD TO FIGHT MY WAY into the game. There were no girls' teams or leagues when I was a kid. Hockey was for boys, I kept hearing, and its coaches and organizers kept coming up with fresh excuses to bar me from playing. That lit a fire in me. I set out to prove to those people trying to keep me out that I belonged, that I was good enough, that they needed me. I spent hours alone on the little rink my dad built behind the house, running through stickhandling and shooting drills, skating sprints, sharpening my game little by little.

But motivation is not a one-step fix. Using the fire inside you to keep pushing yourself is a great first step, but that alone is not enough to get you to the top. I've never seen a teammate get fired up by a loss or a bag skate and then immediately sit down to write a to-do list for their week ahead. But those smaller habits and choices are just as important.

Success, to me, is the aggregate of every single thing you do, every decision you make, big or small, every time you persevere and don't give in to the pain, every good habit you develop. Some of these habits—like showing up on time or trying to win each day—aren't exactly original. But over time, these small, seemingly low-stakes decisions will make all the difference.

These days, I get the chance to meet a lot of young players. The single question that they ask most often—whether it's a little girl or a rookie trying to crack an NHL roster for the first time—is What does it take to make it to the show? My answer is always the same. You have to be willing to do the work when no one is watching.

That's what the first section of this book is about: the hard work I did when no one was watching. The building blocks that seeded my success and built the foundation for my game and my life. I had to get mentally tough. I had to learn to lose. I studied hockey as though I were earning a PhD in the game.

In hockey, the defensive zone relies on discipline and systems. So does this first section. Most of these lessons are small strategies you can use on the daily to get yourself where you want to be.

I.

LOSING ISN'T FAILURE

You learn more from losses than victories

To the day I die, I will never forget how I felt standing at the blue line during the medal ceremony in Nagano, 1998. It was the first Olympics to include women's ice hockey as a sport, and everyone expected Canada to take gold. It was *my* first Olympics.

We got pasted in the final, losing 3–1 to the Americans to bring home the silver. In every photo of that medal ceremony, I'm gazing up at a spot in the rafters, biting my lip, saying to myself, *Get me the hell out of here.* And *I'm not going to let those god-damn Americans see me cry.* I did my crying later. I never wanted to feel that way again. Ever. I think every player standing on our blue line felt that way. As soon as I got off the ice, I took off the medal, folded it up, and put it in the pocket of my coat. I've never worn it since. For years I rarely showed it to anyone. I was so ashamed of it. I hated it.

I've never been a good loser, whether playing crib, knee hockey, or baseball. Hockey has taught me a number of lessons, but the greatest one might be how much we gain by losing. It took me a while after Nagano before I understood that, though.

I showed up to my first national team camp at 15 with a bad haircut and bright red cheeks. The camp was called to prepare us for the '94 World Championships in Lake Placid, New York. My teammates immediately nicknamed me High-Chair Hayley. The oldest player there was 35. My roommate, Margot Page, taught high school math; at the time, I was studying grade 10 math.

You might imagine I felt out of place walking into that dressing room. Being a decade younger than most of the other players. Being a high-schooler whose greatest responsibilities were homework and unloading the dishwasher when nearly all the other women had careers, families, driver's licences. The truth is, I had never been happier. At that age, I knew only a few girls who played hockey. Suddenly I was surrounded by an entire team of women, vicious competitors who could knock the snot out of me and shoot just as hard.

Being around those women at that impressionable age had a huge impact—they showed me how to be a true professional. I saw how much they sacrificed to play the game, scheduling work shifts around tournaments, walking away from jobs when their bosses refused to accommodate their hockey careers. Some things have changed since '94, but the reality of life as a female amateur athlete is still far from glamorous. Your sport doesn't pay your bills. Most players need to have a full-time job to cover rent and living expenses, then spend all of their "spare" time training and competing.

Danielle Goyette, a self-taught player from Saint-Nazaire, Quebec, who became a good friend of mine and later was my coach at the University of Calgary, took a job scrubbing toilets at the Olympic Oval in Calgary to make ends meet. Later, she worked nights at Home Depot, lacing up her steel-toed boots to work in the plumbing section after training all day. The reality is that striving for a career on the national team often means putting your professional career, and earning capacity, on the back burner.

We won those Worlds in '94, and I notched my first point for Team Canada—an assist. I knew it was just the beginning of my time playing for our national team. Once I had my first taste of that level of competition, I couldn't let it go.

As an international sport, women's hockey wasn't well recognized at that point. Prior to Nagano, Canada's national team had played only a half-dozen tournaments sanctioned by the International Ice Hockey Federation (IIHF). I vividly remember watching the inaugural Women's World Hockey Championship in Ottawa in 1990 from my parents' basement. The Canadian team came out dressed in hot-pink jerseys and white satin pants as a publicity stunt. The country's sports journalists (almost all of them men) had been studiously ignoring the tournament, which threatened to be a massive flop. The jerseys were a last-minute ploy to grab their attention and get fans in the stands. I despised those jerseys. To me, all they said was that women's hockey wasn't a real sport. That female hockey players representing our country didn't deserve to wear our country's colours. We had a long way to go before we would be considered legit.

All that changed with Nagano. Granted, the jerseys had already been redesigned by the time I was in the Team Canada system, but the Japanese Olympics were a watershed moment for the women's game. People around the world who didn't even know that women played hockey were exposed to stars like Cammi Granato and Manon Rhéaume. After 1998, girls grew up in a world where they could occasionally see female players in Nike commercials or smiling up at them from cereal boxes. Their heroes no longer needed to be named Mario or Wayne but Cammi and Manon. We were on our way up.

In the fall of '97, I was 18 and one of 28 players invited to centralize in Calgary to compete for spots on Canada's first-ever Olympic women's hockey roster. For six months, we bunked together, trained together, and practised daily. Before then, we sometimes didn't even get a chance to practise as a team before major international tournaments. Players lived all over the country, and it was difficult—and expensive—to get us all together in the same place to work out as a team.

Going into Nagano, Canada was considered unbeatable. We'd won all four IIHF Women's World Hockey Championships held since 1990. Our team's dominance bled over into my personal life, too—I was feeling pretty unstoppable. I had been MVP of my bantam AAA team and of the Calgary Oval X-Treme at the recent Esso Women's National Championship. I'd been named top batter and all-star shortstop at the midget softball nationals. Both times I had represented Canada on the ice in World Championships, I had brought home gold. By the time I got to Japan, the idea that we might lose had never crossed my mind. Not once.

And Nagano wasn't only our first Olympics; it was also the first time NHLers were allowed to skate at the Games. All these guys I'd grown up idolizing—Wayne Gretzky, Steve Yzerman,

Brett Hull, Chris Chelios—were wandering around the venues and the athletes' village, there for the same reason as me.

Japan felt like a different universe—I couldn't believe how busy and crowded the cities felt. It was my first time outside North America. Before Nagano, I'd left Canada twice: for a road trip to Disneyland in California with my family and to Lake Placid, New York, for the '94 World's. The Japanese were as new to hockey as I was to travel. Before faceoffs, the scoreboard would flash "Face Off, Face Off, Face Off" while trance music blared from the speakers. It was exciting, exhilarating, and a hell of a lot of fun.

We won the first four games of the round robin by a margin of 24–5 before meeting the U.S. Since both our teams had clinched spots in the final, the media labelled our round robin game "meaningless," which spoke to how little people outside the sport understood the stakes of women's hockey. We didn't have an NHL to play in. This was the highest level of competition we ever faced. This was our Stanley Cup. Every single game we played against the Americans was important.

We charged to an early 4–1 lead in that "meaningless" game. It was a chippy, rough game—games against the U.S. always are. Towards the end of the second period, the Americans came roaring back, somehow scoring six unanswered goals in the last half of the game. The final score was 7–4, completely humiliating us.

The brutal loss, just three days ahead of the final, rattled us. We had never lost to Team USA at a major international tournament before. Suddenly, we were anxious, nervous. We started questioning decisions. We were flooded with doubt at exactly the wrong moment.

There was more pain to come. This time, it wasn't about our play on the ice. Danielle Goyette, one of our top vets, was playing through unimaginable loss that Olympics; the night before the Opening Ceremonies, her father, Henri-Paul, had died. This was two short years after she had lost her mom to a heart attack. She was shattered and wanted to fly home; her sisters ultimately convinced her to stay and play on. In the handshakes after the loss to the U.S., Goyette thought she heard a U.S. player make an ugly comment about her dad. Our coach, Shannon Miller, who'd been the one to break the news to Danielle that her father had died 10 days earlier, disclosed the taunt to the CBC after the game. It "was uncalled for and Goyette started bawling," Miller added. "That was a big mistake." The U.S. player acknowledged that she had said something in the heat of the moment to Goyette, but that it had nothing to do with her father.

This unleashed a big controversy, with media around the world following each new wrinkle in the story. We'd never had to deal with outside distractions like this before. The dispute was one more thing we were unprepared to handle. And it made for an even more intense final game.

It's hard all these years later to explain just how much excitement—and pressure—surrounded us going into that final. It was the height of the late '90s "Girl Power," and here we were, crashing the men's game. Sportswriters who had spent years ignoring us now couldn't get enough of us. We were on the front pages of North American newspapers. Frustrated reporters were clamouring for a fresh quote. Japanese media were treating Vicky Sunohara, whose grandparents had been raised near Nagano, like a rock star. Filmmakers had spent months and months shadowing us across North America for the National Film Board documentary *The Game of Her Life*. It was like being dropped into a fishbowl after years of obscurity.

We were totally unprepared for the attention and had no idea how to deal with controversy. And we definitely didn't know how to handle constant demands from media and sponsors, or the intense pressure of the Olympic stage. The cracks began to show.

We played Team USA in the first-ever women's hockey gold medal final in front of a full house. It was a major moment for the women's game. Walking out through the tunnel and seeing everyone screaming and waving flags for *warm-up* was unreal. *Holy smokes*, I thought to myself. *I'm playing in a gold medal game. This is really happening!*

The first period ended in a scoreless tie. The U.S. managed eight shots to our nine. It was tough, physical hockey. But we couldn't get any flow. We were playing as individuals. You could see our nerves and our desperation out there. We were playing scared. We were high-strung. Too tight.

Things started to tip in the Americans' favour with less than a minute to go in the second. Nancy Drolet was called for tripping after trying to stop Tara Mounsey from taking a shot. The U.S. suddenly had a power play. Their PP at the time was unreal. We almost managed to kill the penalty, but with just six seconds remaining, Gretchen Ulion scored, putting the U.S. up 1–0.

For the next 10 minutes, we went back and forth. Then Goyette was called for bodychecking. The U.S. went back on the power play. With 9:03 left in the game, Shelley Looney, who was squatting in Manon's crease, sneaked one past her, making it 2–0.

With four minutes left, we cut the lead to one with a goal from Goyette, the tournament's leading scorer. This breathed new life into us. The coaches pulled Manon to give us the extra attacker. We needed just one goal to make it into overtime. But with eight seconds remaining on the clock, Sandra Whyte sailed a 40-footer into the empty net, making the final score 3–1. The clock ran out. In that instant, women's hockey came into its own. But for all of us on Team Canada, that seminal moment felt crushing.

A silver medal might seem like an amazing accomplishment. But for athletes, you never win silver. You lose gold. And for me, and my sport, there was no other award—no playoffs, no Stanley Cup, no all-star game, no awards show. This was it.

When we got back to our dressing room, Stacy Wilson, our captain, played "O Canada," since we hadn't had the chance to sing it on the ice. She wanted us to take pride in all that we had accomplished, even if it wasn't the outcome we so badly wanted. She got us all to stand up on the benches and hold hands. I didn't want to sing. I wasn't proud. I was embarrassed. I wanted to crawl into a corner and die.

I sank into a deep depression once I got back home. I was angry. Angry with myself and the world. I had wanted to succeed so badly, I had expected us to succeed. Coming home without the gold felt like the ultimate failure. Like everything I had worked for was now worthless. It ate away at me. I couldn't sleep. I felt a burning shame inside me. I didn't see my friends, my family.

I was living in a little rented townhouse in Calgary with my teammate and friend Judy Diduck, a defenceman from Sherwood Park. Judy, who is 13 years older than me, handled the loss a whole lot better than I did. She had a healthier perspective and was able to bounce back from it. I tried to deal with my depression on my own. I wasn't holed up in the house drowning my sorrows or off on a partying rampage. The way I dealt with the loss was to throw myself back into my training, working harder than ever—so hard that I didn't have time to stop and think and feel. I was determined never to lose a big game like that again. Judy, on the other hand, had zero desire to start training again. She wanted some time off. It put a strain on our friendship, further isolating me.

At 19, I had no one in my life aside from my teammates. I was this focused, determined athlete who didn't have much in the way of perspective or other interests. If I'd slowed down long enough to think about it, I probably would have realized that I was lonely.

I couldn't wrap my head around the loss: I couldn't separate my failure on the ice from who I was as a person. It left me questioning my self-worth. When we were winning, I felt successful, worthy. If I wasn't an Olympic gold medallist and top-shelf athlete, then who was I? What was I?

Six months after returning from Japan, the coach for my club team, the Calgary Oval X-Treme, Wally Kozak, decided I had struggled long enough. Or maybe it had gotten too hard for him to watch, day after day, my continuing inability to get past the loss. I've known Wally, a fellow Saskie, since I first attended his hockey school as a 12-year-old, and we remain very close.

He took me aside and handed me a piece of paper on which he had written a simple message: "Dear Hayley, A gold medal is a wonderful thing. But if you're not enough without it, you'll never be enough with it."

Somewhere along the way, I had unconsciously decided that once I had the gold medal around my neck, my life would change for the better. That it would fill me with the sense of self-worth and belonging that I had been yearning for. Somehow, the gold would erase all the pain, self-doubt, and loneliness my early life in hockey had bred in me.

Wally was also sending me a warning: if I only cared about gold medals, I was going to miss out on really living my life. He was telling me that it was okay to keep working towards my goals. But if I wasn't happy, the gold medal wouldn't change a thing. He was gently pushing me to get my head out of my ass and figure it out. It hit me like a ton of bricks.

(Wally is a brilliant man and educator, but he has never pretended to be a wordsmith. Years later, he told me that he'd pulled the quote from *Cool Runnings*, a biopic of the Jamaican bobsled team that competed in the '88 Winter Olympics in Calgary and captured the hearts of so many around the world. The quote is something that the bobsled team's coach says to Derice Bannock, the team's heart and soul. When Wally saw that I needed help to get out of my funk, his mind flicked to that moment in the film.)

Reflecting on that period in my life now, I can see that I had a deep fear of failing. Of feeling again the way I did after Nagano. I dug so deep into training as a way to prevent myself from having to experience that kind of heartache again.

The culture of sports is all about winning. It's the "only thing," according to legendary football coach Vince Lombardi. With respect to Mr. Lombardi, on this, he is wrong. No matter how hard you work, no matter how many hours you log in the gym, no matter what you have pushed through and overcome, losing will catch up with you. As it does to all of us. The world of sports, like life itself, is a game of odds. Whether it's in sports or business or relationships, from time to time we fall short.

Losing the gold medal in Nagano showed me the perils of tying my identity to success on the ice. Basing my self-worth on winning would only lead to a very lonely and unhappy life. My perspective didn't change overnight; it was something I had to work on for a really long time. Eventually, with the help of many mentors and years of experience, I was able to separate who I was as a hockey player from the outcome on the ice. I stopped playing with only the outcome in mind, and I focused on the joy of it, on controlling what I could (my play) and letting go of the rest.

Years after Nagano, I had dinner with Mark Messier, who shared with me that throughout his career, he thought as much about losing as he did about winning. Mark stressed that you need to focus on winning, but you can't ignore the possibility of losing. By always preparing for a loss, it never came as a complete shock to him. He anticipated beforehand what it would feel like so that whatever the outcome, he knew he could handle it. Sometimes, he wondered if his life would really be any different if he lost a game, a series, even the Stanley Cup. I was so impressed by how his self-worth wouldn't change if he didn't have those accomplishments on his resumé. His identity was his identity, no matter the outcome of a big game.

Doing your absolute best and working your ass off never guarantees that you will win. In the game of hockey, weird stuff sometimes happens. In 2011, we lost the World Championship to the Americans in Zurich. We outshot and outplayed them. It was an incredible performance. The gold should have been ours. But the game went into overtime and we lost in a shootout. A shootout! What a crapshoot. But that's hockey. And when you think about it, that's life. It can be a tough thing to accept—that after all the hard work, all the preparation, all the long hours and years of work, sometimes you still lose. You can do everything right. The simple fact is, you can't control everything. And your happiness can't hinge on an outcome that may or may not go in your favour.

We tend to frame losing and loss as failure. Something to be avoided at all costs. This is another fallacy I've come to know. In my experience, losing can be the most powerful driving force for winning and success. It's important to remember in those brutal moments when you do fall short that it is not your failures that define you but the way you react to them. It is how you use them to propel change in yourself, to rebound.

The truth is, I learned less from all the gold medal wins and awards than I did from the setbacks, the tough losses, the hardships. When you're winning, you tend to gloss over your flaws, your vulnerabilities, your mistakes. You can start to feel invincible, as I did going into Nagano. Losing, on the other hand, helps us see exactly where our weaknesses lie and how to improve. It's a humbling, painful experience. But ultimately, it's how you get better.

Michael Jordan explained this phenomenon best in a Nike commercial that aired around the time I got back from Japan. I'm a huge Jordan fan, so what he said resonated with me. He'd just returned to the NBA following his retirement from basketball, the murder of his beloved father, and a stint in baseball's minor leagues. He would go on to a second three-peat with the

Chicago Bulls. Twenty-six times his team trusted him to take the game-winning shot and he missed, he says in the ad. In all, Jordan tells us, he missed more than 9,000 shots in his career. He succeeded by failing—over and over again. Not in spite of it. But *because* of it. Learning from your mistakes is how you get better.

Once I opened my eyes to this concept of having to lose before you can win, I saw it everywhere. That there was no shame in trying, in screwing up, and learning from it. It isn't failure at all, just winning in progress. I caught a highlight reel with my dad one night, and we watched a spectacular goal from Jaromir Jagr. "Oh my gosh, how does he do that?" I asked my dad. "It's a beautiful goal, no doubt," he replied. "But I betcha he tried that move nine times before and it failed. And that was the one time that it actually worked."

Not only did Wally's note give me the perspective I needed; it also helped me transform my fear of failing into a pursuit of greatness. It became an obsession, our team's obsession. The first thing we did after Nagano was take stock of what had gone wrong, and it was pretty simple. We choked as a team. We underperformed. We missed wide-open nets and passes to open players. When we fell behind, we didn't stick together. We were all trying too hard to do it ourselves. We were too tight, and we let the pressure get to us. The Americans, on the other hand, played loose and free and as one.

Our coaching staff wasn't experienced enough to understand how to help us navigate all the new expectations that had been heaped on us. I don't blame them for it. Shannon Miller was the first woman coaching at that level. She didn't get a lot of support, and she did the best she could with the few resources she had. The organization had kept us in a bubble throughout the Games, isolating us from our parents, our partners, our friends. Shannon thought it would lessen the pressure we were feeling. Instead of calming us down and keeping us focused, it had the opposite effect: we felt like we were living inside a pressure cooker. We were locked in our rooms, seeing no one but our teammates, thinking of nothing but the upcoming final. But Shannon couldn't have anticipated that.

The Americans, meanwhile, had taken an entirely different tack. We saw them in the athletes' village getting haircuts and massages, soaking up the Olympic experience. They went sightseeing with their families. They hung out at the arcade. They didn't appear tense. They seemed to be having a blast. As we saw in the gold medal game, that looseness eased the pressure off them and freed them to perform at their best.

At the next Olympics in Salt Lake, our coaching staff welcomed our families. They knew it was important to keep the atmosphere light and positive between games. They encouraged us to watch other sports, to enjoy the Olympic experience, and they allowed us a lot of freedom away from the rink. In those games, I was named tournament MVP and was the top scorer.

After Nagano, we analyzed how and why we had fallen short and learned from our mistakes. We didn't lose another championship game for the next seven years.

It's hard to focus on failing forward when the pain of a loss is so fresh. But every time I have fallen, I've grown stronger, grittier, and more resilient.

The reason I was at Nagano in the first place was due to a failure, or what had felt like one at the time. A few months before the tryouts for Team Canada, I was playing boys' midget AAA hockey in Alberta. I am still the only girl to ever do so. Fifteen games into our season, my team took a road trip. I had a great tournament. When our bus dropped us at our home rink in Calgary, the coach called me into his office. I thought he was going to say "Great job out there," or tell me he was moving me onto the power play. Instead, he looked me in the eye and said: "You're a great hockey player but I'm going to have to let you go. I can't handle having a girl on the team. I'm sorry." None of the other coaches stood up for me. No one said, "Hey, this isn't right."

I was devastated. I could play at that level. Though I eventually healed from the hurt, it left a scar. To this day, I still wince every time I drive past that arena.

The thing is, getting cut also lit a fire in me. I had something to prove. I was still seething with anger at Team Canada tryouts a few months later. I was flying out there. The next time that coach saw me play, I was wearing red and white in Nagano. That felt amazing.

Learning from your mistakes to get better is incredibly valuable, but failure is also a great motivator. The best players in the world aren't afraid to fail. It just makes them chase success harder. Take Michael Jordan again: he was famously cut from his high school basketball team. He didn't sit back and give up—he tried harder. When he was working out and felt tired, he used to think of the roster hanging in the dressing room without his name on it. That pushed him onward. The people who can keep getting back up after they fall down, who can persevere, are the ones who end up going all the way.

I used the loss in Nagano as motivation, the same way MJ used the experience of not making the varsity squad as a high-schooler. Shortly after returning to Calgary from Japan, I got an invite to attend the Philadelphia Flyers training camp. It came from Bob Clarke, the team's general manager. Bob, who has since become a mentor and dear friend, had also been the general manager of the men's Olympic team. He'd watched me play in Japan and thought I was good enough to skate with his rookies, who were the same age as me.

A lot of players would have declined the challenge and opted for some downtime instead. It was right after an intense Olympics. But I wasn't interested in time off. I wanted to fail forward. I felt that bringing my game to another level was the best way to do it.

In today's NHL, development camps are used to educate players about systems and training programs and to set them up for the rest of training. Most players have already been on the ice for several weeks by the time dev camps start up. In the '90s, NHL development camps got the players into game shape. The goal was to break us down and build us back up again.

Philly's rookie camp was intense. We had two ice times a day and another off-ice session in the weight room and on the track. I would get up at 6 a.m. and fall into bed about 8 p.m. every night, beat up and exhausted. I loved every minute of it. It gave me a huge physical advantage when I came back to the women's game.

Failures aren't limited to the world of sports, nor are the lessons we can learn from them. I certainly needed these lessons when I was applying to med school. People sometimes assume that, because of my public profile, getting into medical school and studying to become a doctor must have been a cakewalk for me. Nothing could be further from the truth. I applied twice before I got in. But I didn't let the rejection deter me. I didn't take it personally; I didn't give up. I told myself it was a numbers game: almost everyone applying to med school has awesome grades and a kick-ass CV, but not everyone is willing to keep trying. I tweaked my application and applied again, and again. Finding out I'd finally been accepted was a deeply emotional experience. Particularly since I was pretty sure that I'd flubbed my interview.

When you're interviewing for a spot in a medical school, they run you through a series of stations with members of the department. At my very last station, I was asked why I wanted to go into medicine, a deceptively simple question.

At the time, I was recovering from a terrible injury—I was wearing a cast from my knee to my toes. I was exhausted and in pain. When the last physician interviewing me asked why I wanted to go into medicine, I started reflecting back on my journey. I thought of my son, of the little girl from my hometown whose accident had led me to consider becoming a doctor, of how much and for how long I had been dreaming of being a doctor and how scared I was that my application would be rejected again—and I broke down in tears. It was completely unexpected. The physician sitting across from me handed me a box of Kleenex. I dried my eyes and got through his question the best I could before hobbling off, figuring I'd completely blown it.

I was accepted.

Years later, I was sitting in the departure lounge at Toronto Pearson International Airport, waiting to board a flight to Calgary, when a funny thing happened. A man came up to me and introduced himself; he was the doctor who'd interviewed me at the final station.

"I don't know what came over me," I said. "I didn't expect to cry at all." Before we boarded our flight, I asked him whether my tears had harmed my chances. "Not at all," he said. "I loved it. In that moment, you were so real."

He didn't see my fear of failure and emotional outburst as shortcomings or reasons why I wouldn't make a good doctor. Rather than harming his perception of me, it endeared me to him. Failure, and the fear of it, comes for all of us. What matters is what we do with it.

Losing the gold at my first Olympics changed my life. I learned so tangibly (and devastatingly) early on that failure is not fatal. It stings. It sucks. But I came to see that failure is the setup for a comeback. The losses just inspire you to do better. To work harder. To learn from your mistakes.

To this day, I carry Wally's note with me in my wallet everywhere I go. On dark days, it helps lift me back up. It's a reminder to never let failure define me. I can accept it. I can learn from it. I can use it as a springboard to propel me to whatever comes next. But I'll never let it defeat me.

- Focus on winning but don't ignore the possibility of losing.

- Cultivating interests and friendships outside work will help you maintain perspective and manage disappointment.

2.

GROW YOUR GRIT

Grit can get it done

"Freak."

"Stay the hell away from my son."

"You don't belong here."

"Go play ringette."

A lot of ugly things were yelled at me and whispered behind my back. When I was growing up, there weren't a lot of other girls in the game. The kids could be bad. Some of the dads, too. But the moms, the small-town gender police, they were the worst.

I cut my hair short: a mushroom cut with a blond wave. It was peak '90s style. You can't blame me for the era's bad fashion trends! And I figured if I had short hair, no one could tell that I was a girl.

I spent hours working on my game on my backyard rink, deking imaginary defencemen, perfecting my wrist shot, my slapshot, stickhandling up and down the tiny surface. I thought if my play was good enough, it could do the talking for me. If I was good enough, people wouldn't criticize me or yell things at me.

Boy, was I wrong.

The way they saw it, now I was taking the shine off someone's son, hogging *their* ice time, nabbing *their* roster spot. Some people resented the attention I drew, the talent I had. By the time I was in bantam, it was so toxic that at age 15, I developed an ulcer. The constant stress and anxiety were tearing me up inside. On the ice, I was a target. Guys took runs at me. Coaches goaded their players into putting me in my place. I'd climb into my dad's car after games all banged up and bruised. It was hard for him to watch.

When I was the first woman to skate in a men's pro league, the target appeared on my back all over again. I had to fight for my right to be there. I never once felt welcome in men's leagues. Still, I kept pushing to be included.

In the face of that persistence, people eventually stopped saying no. It was grit that got me through the rink door. Resilience is what kept me there.

I've come to know grit as my greatest strength. It's what got me to the top of my game, and it's how I built my career after retiring. It's the foundation for success. The good news is grit and resilience aren't attributes that you either have or don't have. They're like muscles that you can strengthen and grow.

Grit and resilience are two sides of the same coin. When you're tired, you have to dig deep. Grit is putting in the time when no one else is, when no one is watching. It's doing the shit you don't want to do but that you know will make you better. Grit is staying behind an extra 20 minutes to finish up a patient's chart.

It's going for a morning run after being up all night with a colicky baby. Grit is pure work. It has propelled me forward even when I felt like I had nothing left to give.

Resilience is the ability to keep going, to keep doing something again and again—it's the repetition of grit over time. Anyone can be gritty in a moment. Not everyone can do it over and over again for years. Resilience is what separates good athletes from great athletes. Steeled by it, they are able to overcome failure, stress, media pressure, and negative public opinion. Resilience is a combination of backbone and self-discipline. It's a state of mind that gives you the strength to keep reaching, to keep getting back up when you fall down. Resilience is about overcoming.

I got my grit from my grandfather, John Eberts. Grandpa ran a pristine grain and cattle farm in Saskatchewan for 60 years. He loved farming: the animals and the outdoors, the satisfaction of seeing a job done well, the meditation in repeating the same motions over and over, the way he felt after a long, hard day. Growing up, I used to chase him all over the farm. Wherever he went, I followed. Whatever he was tinkering with, so was I. He's the only person I've known who loved to work hard as much as I do. I learned *from* him how to love work as much as he did.

The years of labour weren't easy on his body. I'll never forget my grandfather's giant, rock-strong hands. I keep a picture of them on my phone. Each finger was as wide as a piano key. They were chapped and bent, bearing the scars of decades of hard work in driving winds and sub-zero temperatures. But that day-in, day-out labour of hauling buckets, lifting calves, moving fence posts builds muscles you can't get at a gym. The strength he built over decades was unmatched. People tell stories about how Gordie Howe built his muscles doing farm work and working construction, how he never picked up a weight at a gym—I was never surprised hearing that. I saw that same strength in Grandpa. I've met more first-round draft picks than I can name, yet my grandfather remains the strongest person I have ever known.

Grandpa was also gentle and kind and fun-loving. He was deeply involved with the community. He played banjo and the accordion and loved to sing and entertain. He was the life of every party and the glue that bound our family together.

I wanted to be just like him. He always seemed to know what he was doing, to have a purpose for each day. He was always in control. Spending my days beside him made me feel that way, too. I wanted to be as strong as he was. When I wasn't holding wrenches or hammers for him, I'd load up his rusty wheelbarrow with heavy rocks and lie beneath it so that I could bench-press the handles. That was my first set of weights. I saw how at peace and happy Grandpa was doing manual labour. It seemed like so much more to him than work. Like his mind was free and easy because his body was busy. In adulthood, I find I do my best thinking when my body is working, a moving meditation.

Grandpa gave me my first lessons in grit and pushing past my limits. He felt that if a person could command a horse, they could do almost anything in life. The only trouble was, I was dead scared of them. His horses were these great big animals who whinnied and snorted and pounded their heavy hooves, kicking up dirt. That was terrifying to five-year-old me. I had good reason to be afraid: their hooves were bigger than my head.

Or at least they looked that way at the time. Grandpa decided that I would get over my fear if I learned to ride.

You might be picturing a gentle grandfather lifting a small, scared child onto the back of a saddled pony. That isn't what happened. Grandpa was kind as hell, but he also believed that diving into the deep end was the best way to learn. He lifted me onto a horse standing in the corral—no saddle or reins. "Hang on" was all he said. He must have given the horse's rump a good slap because it took off at full gallop. I held on for dear life, gripping its mane with my fingers and leaning on its neck.

I have no idea how long the horse ran for. I was doing everything in my power to keep from falling off. At some point, the horse must've decided it was done running and wandered back to the barn, where Grandpa lifted me off.

After surviving that ride, horses weren't so terrifying anymore. I was thrown into the deep end and didn't drown. Grandpa didn't teach me to get over my fear with words but by showing me what I was capable of. That day, he showed me that I could handle far more than I thought. It's just one way you can grow grit: taking on things that feel way beyond you. Now, I probably wouldn't stick a kindergartner on a horse—even one wearing a saddle and *reins*—but I agree with the essence of Grandpa's lesson. You don't know what you are capable of until you challenge yourself. Every time I get the chance, I put myself in tough or uncomfortable situations. They force me to dig deep, to figure out how to push through. Would I have gotten over my fear of horses if Grandpa had put me on a small, saddled pony and eased me into it? Maybe. But it wouldn't have made me feel as invincible as I did that day.

Those memories I have of Grandpa are still crystal clear, decades later. I honestly think those lessons I learned at five years old have had the most impact on my career. "You have to be willing to do things that other people aren't," he used to tell me. He always said that I could do anything, I just had to be willing to outwork everyone else. Grandpa believed that you had to fall down before you could get back up again. No matter what, you could always find a way through. He gave me a foundation of grit, and I've been building on it ever since.

It takes a combination of a lot of things to be successful, and you need grit to get all those other things done. There is a lot more to grit than the monumental-but-fleeting feeling of success when you achieve what you didn't think was possible. A lot of grit is very, very, very boring. It's long hours and tedious work building that grit, building that resilience, and pushing through to your goals. Which is where resilience comes in, performing grit day in and day out.

Anyone can work hard for a day or a game. But most people give up when it gets really tough.

I don't know if Team Canada was ever the most talented team at any Olympics I attended. But when we were backed into a corner, we would not stop. We refused to give up. This wasn't some inherent talent we had; we cultivated this culture as a team and pushed ourselves over and over and over until we had the grit we needed to succeed.

In the summer before every Winter Olympics, Team Canada kicked off centralization with six weeks together in a tortuous boot camp, and then we spent the next six months in Calgary.

At camp, our days began with a team run at 6 a.m. and often didn't end until after 9 p.m. Hockey Canada designs these camps to get us out of our comfort zones. On top of skating and weight training, we would go rock climbing, hiking, and dragon boat racing. We did our own form of duathlons and triathlons. We ran obstacle courses wearing heavy backpacks in 35 degree Celsius heat. It's not just the range of activities but the sheer volume of them that tested our limits. There were always a lot of tears and yelling, even vomiting. It's a grind from start to finish. Everyone broke down at some point during the camp. It was pretty much a given and part of the process.

The idea is that if you can get through the hell of camp, you'll be able to push through anything that might come up at the Games. Boot camp is also meant as a wake-up call. A lot of the players might think they were training hard in the off-season, but when they get to camp, they realize what hard work actually looks like.

On the last day of one of these camps, we were in Penticton, B.C. At 6 a.m., our usual time, we arrived at the parking lot outside the rink, our morning meeting spot. We were exhausted, dying to get home. Our coaching staff told us that we'd be cycling from the parking lot to the peak of the Apex Mountain before we could leave.

Just looking at that mountain, I knew we were in for a tough climb, but my heart sank to my stomach when the equipment manager rattled up towing a U-Haul full of the oldest, crappiest, most beat-up bikes I had ever seen. Apex is a Tour de France–ranked climb. You should never ride up that beast on anything less than a lightweight, high-quality road bike. We were being handed big, old, heavy mountain bikes. Did I mention it was raining sideways and cold as hell that day? It was coming down so hard that we weren't even allowed to descend the mountain after the race; it would have been too dangerous.

We were frozen, sore, and cranky. We missed our families. We were sick and tired of each other. We'd been at camp for weeks, running, lifting weights, getting bag skated. We were done. But the job was not. So, we had to dig deep.

I wanted to leave camp on a high note. I wanted to push myself to the max. Cycling was my wheelhouse. I wanted to set an example. I jammed my earphones in my ears and told myself, *I'm going to suffer until I get to the top of this mountain, and I'm going to enjoy the suffering, because I know that somewhere down the road, this is going to pay off.* I stayed completely in the moment and took it one pedal stroke at a time. Reaching that peak made the pain fade away, as did the knowledge that we had once again raised our limits as a team.

That is how you grow your grit. By trying. By failing. By doing it over. By stepping back and finding a better way to do it. Then doing that again. And again. And probably again. Over time, grit becomes resilience.

It's like the calluses I remember on my grandpa's hands. When he was pulling a rope with his bare hands or pushing the tractor into a gear that didn't want to catch, it would have stung and cut his hands at first. But over time, calluses built up, allowing him to keep going until the job was done. Calluses are outward signs of resilience.

Resilience is trainable. As an athlete, I was always building my internal resilience reserves. It made the big game or the key shift less stressful because I knew that the training I'd done in preparation had been so much harder. I trained so hard that the games were easy in comparison and I had reserves to draw on.

My training routine was pretty intense when I was playing, even by Olympic standards. I'd put in two, three hours at the gym on easy days. Sometimes I got in trouble with Team Canada staff for working out too hard or doing extra skating drills. But it was some of the more unique training I did that really raised the bar for me and built those calluses.

Every summer, "Jungle" Jim Hunter, an alpine skier from the Crazy Canuck era, used to lead me on a 600-kilometre road ride from Calgary to Nelson, B.C., with his nephews. (Back then, his five nephews were farmers and aspiring hockey players. These days, they are rising country music stars, known as the Hunter Brothers in Nashville and beyond.) We would ride for three days straight, stopping only to rest and eat—and occasionally puke—on the side of the road. It was some of the hardest training I ever did; there were times I felt like I was gonna pass out on my bike. It was damn hot and almost impossible to maintain the pace.

Jungle Jim used to drive behind us on the highway in a minivan, to protect us. He'd shout instructions and encouragement from the window. Not that we could hear or understand anything he was saying! He even fed us from the minivan. He'd put energy bars and chocolate in the scoop of a lacrosse stick and reach it out the window. We'd roll up beside him and grab them.

After three days, we would hit Nelson and throw our bikes in the lake as a celebration—then climb into the back of the van and drive straight back to Calgary, where we kept training. The day after we got back, Jim would have us pushing boulders up hills, scrambling up rocky peaks, and jumping off picnic tables. It was ugly, gritty training and I absolutely loved it. It's still my favourite way to train.

The point was to do something so hard and so intense that you force your mind to go somewhere else, allowing your body to push beyond what you thought you were capable of. It steels you. In driving myself into the ground I was developing resilience, the flip side of the grit coin. I learned to push through fatigue. I wasn't just steeling my body; Jim used to say that we were also steeling our minds. And the mind is a hell of a lot stronger than the body.

If you are constantly training the hardest you possibly can, the games become easy. This style of training was all about hardening myself, raising the bar physically and mentally so that playing in a normal environment wouldn't feel that hard. If you raise the bar every day in training, by the time you get to the gold medal game, you don't need to raise it any higher. You've already gotten to that next level. You've been competing there every single day. I felt like it gave me a huge mental advantage over my opponents, as well. I knew that very few would put their body and mind through what I had.

It took me a while to truly start enjoying this sort of extreme and constant limit-pushing. When I was younger, I saw work as a means to a goal. I lifted weights to get stronger, skated sprints to get faster, studied the game to get smarter, put in effort towards a goal that was always just out of my reach. It wasn't sustainable. Having a goal to chase is great motivation, but it's hard to maintain when you're always stretching but never reaching it. Over time, I came to understand that chasing a dream had to be about more than seeking a result. It wasn't enough for me to keep pushing my limits every day. Genuinely enjoying the work I did day in, day out—that was my turning point. When I started to love throwing weights around simply for the joy and satisfaction it brought me—not doing it for the farther-off goal of getting stronger—I came to love the process. The work became a way of life for me. It became a joy for me, as it was for Grandpa.

To this day, I am happiest when I'm on a 100-kilometre bike ride. I love the pain, the burning sensation in the pit of my lungs. This is how I express my passion. This is who I am. The truth is, none of it feels like work to me.

Constantly pushing your limits up and up might sound really intense, but your mind and body are miraculous systems. The conscious mind can't distinguish mental from physical stimuli, so if you keep telling yourself that you're not tired, eventually your mind will start to believe it.

I've found that it's important to be gentle with myself. When I was younger, I used to beat myself up a lot, criticizing myself in my head. I could be brutal. As I got older, I learned how important it is to be your own best friend. Even when it feels like the world is not on your side—or maybe especially then. I learned to give myself the reassurance that I needed to keep going.

When I'm fighting with my body, I bargain with myself, almost the same way I would if I was negotiating to buy a house. I make the first offer. I use concrete numbers. I refuse to bend. If I was feeling super hungry but was too slammed to eat, I might say to myself, *Okay, hunger, I feel you. But I need you to go away for the next two hours. When that time is up, you can come back with full force. And believe me, I will feed you. But right now, I need you to go the hell away.*

Bargaining with myself like this made training a bit easier. *Okay, you need to climb to the top of that hill, then you get a break,* I'd say to myself. *One more wind sprint, then you can hit the shower.* This reduced every training session to a series of short sprints, which felt less daunting, more manageable.

Let me tell you, this trick of negotiating with myself made it easier to balance my career with parenting, especially when my son was an infant. There were so many nights when he would sleep only a couple hours at a time, and it's a monumental task to get your legs going in a game when you've barely slept. During games after staying up all night with a colicky Noah, I'd tell myself: *All right, dear legs. In 15 minutes and 40 seconds when the period is over, you can be as tired as you want for the intermission. But until then, you are going to fly out there. You will feel no pain. You are not tired.*

When I was working in the hospital during the pandemic, I'd psych myself up and mentally prepare for the day ahead by having a little dialogue with the virus. *Today, COVID, you and I are going to meet,* I'd say to myself. *And we are going to go into battle. I'm going to encounter you in patients, and I'm going to work hard to slay you. And at the end of the day we are going to part ways, and I'm going to leave you at work.* I always try to treat myself with kindness. The outside world directs enough anger and pressure at me. I don't need to add to that.

I've never had to rely on my grit more than I have since retiring from hockey. In the summer of 2018, I got a call out of the blue from Kyle Dubas, general manager of the Toronto Maple Leafs, offering me a job as assistant director of player development.

It was a dream job. I hadn't planned on working in the game so soon after retiring from playing. But as much as I wanted to take the position Kyle was offering, I had to tell him the truth: I had just started med school—a lifelong dream of mine. I wasn't willing to give that up.

It turned out he wasn't ready to give up on me either.

A few days later, Kyle and I had a creative discussion over lunch about how the job could work for us both. I asked for a lot: the flexibility to work for the Leafs while also studying medicine. I also needed time to give speeches and make appearances, my main source of income. To be honest, though, managing multiple jobs and responsibilities (and the grit and resilience it requires) was nothing new to me—I'd had a lot of practice.

To no one's surprise, finances for a female athlete look a lot different than they do for male athletes. I played little more than two seasons in pro leagues; for most of my career, I was an amateur athlete, one who didn't receive a salary. I didn't exactly walk away from my playing career with a lot of money.

I moved out of my parents' house when I was 17. I was playing for the Oval X-Treme at the time, sharing an $800-per-month rental with Judy Diduck, the best penny-pincher I ever met. Judy was as cheap as they come, and I mean that as a compliment. She taught me how to get by on very little. She was also one of the best and smartest defencemen to ever lace up for Team Canada. Neither of us had a job outside of the national team; we needed to focus solely on training to be ready for the first Olympics our sport would compete in. We received $800 per month from Sport Canada's Athlete Assistance Program (which funds high-level athletes). Our equipment, physiotherapy, and ice time were covered by Hockey Canada, and we used that stipend to pay for everything else life requires, like rent and groceries. I drove a

Chrysler K-car and had to be extremely careful with gas, never paying for parking unless I absolutely had to. We didn't have extra cash to go to bars or clubs—hell, we didn't have money to go out for dinner or buy furniture that wasn't falling apart. Bars aren't my jam, anyway. We lived simply and got by.

It was really important to me to live independently—I never took money from my parents after I moved out. My parents had already sacrificed everything to put three kids in hockey. When my family first moved to Calgary when I was a kid, my mom and dad didn't have two dimes to rub together. Houses in the city cost twice what they did in rural Saskatchewan. We didn't go on vacations; we would go camping or visit my grandpa on the farm instead. Every extra dollar we had went to paying for hockey trips or hockey school or hockey equipment.

When I got older, I knew I wasn't going to make millions playing. I wasn't going to be able to buy my parents a house, as much as I would have loved to. But what I could do was be financially independent, so they no longer had to support me. When I was on Team Canada, they would spend $15,000 every four years to take my brother and sister to the Olympics for two weeks to cheer me on. It would take them until the next Olympics to repay it.

I was always hustling, and it took about 10 years of patching together gigs and raising my profile before I stopped struggling financially. It's a really common situation for amateur athletes: everyone needs a side hustle to make ends meet and a backup plan for when their athletic career is over. After the '98 Olympics, I started speaking at elementary and high schools and I taught at hockey schools. Speaking in front of people was tough for a shy gal like me! But I took every gig I could to increase the visibility of the women's game and make a bit of money. By that point I could call myself an Olympic athlete, which made me a bit more marketable.

Most female hockey players don't make any real money playing in Canada—unless it's an Olympic year. In those years, Team Canada players are paid $50,000 to $80,000, earning the top dollar if we bring home the gold. But it's feast or famine. In non-Olympic years, female hockey players top out at $18,000 per year from a federal government program, if they are part of the national team program. That's not going to get you very far when the average monthly rent for an apartment in a lot of cities is 10 percent of that. The situation is more dire if you aren't in the national program; women's professional hockey leagues in North America go up and down, and before the National Women's Hockey League that was founded in 2015, most weren't able to pay players. When I played in the Canadian Women's Hockey League before it folded, we even had to pay for our own ice time. And these are numbers from the end of my career; back in the late '90s, we weren't getting a lot of money—or respect—from Hockey Canada.

Olympics take everything you have, including time. In Olympic years, the top 27 players in the country are together in Calgary for the seven and a half months leading up the Games. I lived in Calgary, so I never had to uproot my family, but most of my teammates had to give up a lot in order to play for our country.

Becky Kellar, who lived in Ontario, had to move herself and her two boys to Calgary to centralize. Her husband ran a construction business and had to stay behind, so Becky's mom would come with her to help with the kids while she was training. You can't work during centralization: you're at the rink for six to eight hours a day, six days a week, for over six months. Most of my teammates had to take leaves of absence from their jobs. We needed money to pay for moving expenses, childcare, and living expenses.

None of us was ever looking to get rich. But we needed a way to take a year out of our lives to compete for Canada at the Winter Olympics. The reason we never had to get into the ugly public fights over salaries the way that Team USA's female hockey and soccer players did was because of the Women's High Performance Advisory Committee formed after the Nagano Olympics by such veteran players as France St-Louis, Stacy Wilson, and Thérèse Brisson. They fought to get us compensated in Olympic years.

The highest level of women's sports is staggeringly different from men's. Since we either don't get salaries (making us amateur athletes) or our salaries are so much lower by comparison, women tend to retire with a lot less money but excellent educations, often from the Ivy League colleges they played for. A lot of us put these degrees to use in our 30s, when we hang up our skates. This is a huge advantage the women's game has and something the men's game could learn from; these educations set you up for when you can no longer play. But the women have a lot more to juggle during their playing career than men do. They're not just training and competing and working another job; they are also planning for life after hockey—when they can finally earn a bit of money. Male players have to plan for life after hockey, too, but their salaries make a huge difference in how this looks. They retire with so much more in the bank that they have time to figure things out. A top female hockey player *might* make enough to live on from hockey alone in an Olympic year—but that's one out of every four years.

All this is to say that, being a female amateur athlete takes a lot of grit. When your full-time gig—being on the national team—

doesn't pay you enough to make ends meet three out of four years, you develop a lot of resilience. You get creative. My real earning window, and ability to start saving for retirement, began when I retired from the game and had the time to embark on a second career. My son had started university, and that's why, aside from its being a dream of mine, I chose that time to go to medical school. And then Kyle Dubas threw the most fantastic of wrenches into my plan when he offered me the player development role with the Leafs.

After my conversation with Kyle, I reached out to some doctor friends to see whether they thought I could hack both the Leafs job and med school. Medical school tuition is steep, and the Leafs job would make paying for it a whole lot easier. They all felt that my demeanour, personality, and work ethic would allow me to manage the workload for the first two years. The third year, they all said, would be rough. That final year is brutal because you spend your days with patients, doing clinical rotations as a clerk in hospitals, and your nights studying for the battery of exams you need to graduate. It's a slog, even without a job in the NHL. Without a job outside of school, period.

My friends were right. The first two years of medical school are mostly spent in a lecture hall. These days most lectures get recorded, so I was able to download them onto my phone. I listened on the plane or after I got off the ice with the Leafs. For the first two years, I flew to Toronto four to six times every month. I also worked with Toronto's Western Hockey League prospects in Calgary.

In third year, I also faced a major logistical challenge: the teaching hospitals affiliated with my university are in Alberta. But to maintain my commitment with the Leafs, I needed to complete one-third of my rotations in Ontario. I had to get creative the way I did early in my career and rely on my grit to do whatever it took. I had to carve my own path by pleading my case to the Student Academic Review Committee, which makes final decisions about academic transfers. It was essentially a small trial—and stressful as hell. In the end, they gave me the go-ahead.

Studying medicine is not cheap and working for the Leafs has helped cover some of my bills, but I'm still supplementing that with sponsorships, speaking engagements, and several businesses that I've either helped found or invested in over the years.

As a kid, I was gritty because I had to be. I had to force my way into a game that didn't want me. When I got older, grit helped me stretch the limits of my abilities. I've come to believe that it is my greatest strength, and that it's what made everything else possible. Grit got me to the Olympics. But I had no idea just how much grit would help me after my athletic career was over. Getting through medical school has been more about grit than anything else. There have been days when I didn't think I could keep going. It's been the fucking grind of my life—the most mentally exhausting thing I have ever been through. Thank god I had those calluses that I'd built over the years to help me keep pulling.

- Grit and resilience are two sides of the same coin, and success requires both.
- Grit is putting in the time when no one else is—and when no one else is watching.
- Resilience is the ability to keep going, to keep doing something again and again—it's the repetition of grit over time.

3.

REST IS A WEAPON

Be relentless in your rest

You might think it odd to jump from talking about the importance of grit—of getting up after being knocked down, of always pushing past your limits—directly into the importance of rest. I promise you, it isn't strange at all. Grit requires rest. It is vital to it.

I didn't fully understand how important rest is until my fourth Olympics. What had I been doing before then? I don't even want to think about it. No doubt, running myself ragged. My turning point came one night in 2006, a few weeks before I flew to Italy for the Turin Games. I was standing outside the Saddledome in Calgary after watching the Flames take on the Oilers. I ran into Ryan Smyth as he was getting on Edmonton's bus. We started chatting about life, the weirdness of being an athlete, how difficult it is to find the time to raise a family.

In the previous weeks, even months, I'd been feeling a lot of pressure and stress building inside me. The same thing had happened before Nagano and Salt Lake. Leading up to the Olympics,

I'd hit a lull, a low point. The excitement of having made the roster would be long gone. The training would be difficult, the media and sponsor demands unrelenting. There would be days and weeks where I felt overwhelmed with the expectations, the pressure, the non-stop schedule, the physical fatigue. I would be trying to manage everything but just barely hanging on. I mentioned to Ryan how tired I felt. I said I was burning the candle at both ends, when he cut me off. "Hayley, you can't do that," he said. "Rest is a weapon." That line stopped me cold.

When you are working towards something you desperately want, there is a temptation to go all out, all the time. There is a perception that if you want it badly enough, you'll always be working towards that goal. That busier is better. That rest is for the weak. That stinging on sleep is industrious, even virtuous. That working longer hours, cutting down your rest time, proves how dedicated you are.

The phrase "endless pursuit of your goals" can be misleading: "endless pursuit" implies that there isn't time to rest or reenergize. It implies that you have to always be chasing, be hustling. That time spent resting is unproductive. You can fall into the trap of believing that the only way to work hard is to do it for hours on end. The culture of medicine is especially guilty of this line of thinking: residents often need to put in 16-hour shifts day after day or go sleepless for a 26-hour shift.

When we get caught up in checking things off our lists and chasing our goals, it's easy to overlook the fact that performance *depends* on rest. If you don't give yourself downtime, you will never be able to perform at your best.

Hockey is an explosive game. You can see the importance of rest when you get caught on the ice too long. Your legs turn to cement. You make mistakes. You become unproductive. After all, performance doesn't just come from training. Many of the physical gains you make from training actually come from resting properly, eating properly, sleeping properly. When you don't rest or sleep, your cognition and recovery time drops. The only way to build out your fitness level is by giving your body time to repair and recover: to form new neural pathways, metabolize protein, and build muscle. If you are killing yourself at the gym and never taking the time to recover, you won't be able to reach the next level. The same goes for regular day-to-day existence. It's not-so-common sense.

Working all the time on very little sleep doesn't result in good performance or build character. It causes accidents. When you show up to work exhausted, you might as well be drunk. Going 24 hours without sleep is worse than having a blood alcohol content of 0.1 percent. Not getting enough sleep has been linked to car crashes, medical errors, even industrial disasters. It's a major factor in diabetes, heart disease, and depression as well as behavioural issues in kids. Can you guess the percentage of the population that can perform perfectly on less than six hours sleep? The answer is zero.

When you get enough sleep, on the other hand, you're more likely to feel motivated, light, even joyful. Sleep improves your memory as well as your ability to learn new information, handle problems, even read facial cues. It isn't just about sleep, though; when you spend time away from work to do the things you enjoy, you're a hell of a lot more productive and creative, and less prone to making mistakes. The body and mind are not built to grind it out for days on end.

That's why I love how Ryan framed rest: as a weapon, not a luxury. A means of gaining an advantage, of getting one up over the opposition.

If we can stop equating rest with laziness and instead consider it just as important to achieving our goals as the work itself, it'll be easier to give ourselves time and space for rest. It's the key to performance, and safeguarding rest isn't selfish. It's necessary.

It's a habit I needed to build, something that didn't come naturally to me. Sometimes, I need to be reminded to take care of myself first—before my teammates, my players, even my son. Putting yourself and your needs first is often viewed as selfish, something we are trained not to be, especially as women. It's easy to forget that your primary responsibility is to yourself, not your team or company. That you need to put the oxygen mask on first and take better care of yourself by getting enough sleep, working out, eating right, finding a balance. Taking care of yourself actually isn't selfish, because it gives the people in your life the best of you. A teammate showing up exhausted can't contribute at the level they would if they were rested. If I'm not rested, I'm not doing my best work, and I really feel it. I get irritated. When I'm truly rested, I'm more creative. I get new ideas. Genius lies in the quiet. I learned to let myself go there so I could fully be there for my team, for my son. It also made me a hell of a lot more fun to be around!

To protect my need to rest, I became very deliberate about media and sponsor demands in Olympic years. I had to draw clear boundaries to keep myself from slipping back into old habits.

It wasn't just with my work responsibilities; I was upfront with my parents, my siblings, and my friends as well. I told them they weren't going to see much of me in those years. Fortunately, they were all understanding. I was selfish with my time; I had to be. I fiercely protected my days off. They became a precious time to stop the noise, to get quiet, to be by myself at home, to reenergize. I took it very seriously. I was a pro athlete. And being a pro athlete meant working hard *and* resting hard.

At least in Olympic years, I felt that I had a good excuse for being "selfish" with my time. We were trying to bring back the gold, which was a good reason to say, "No, I can't have dinner with you tonight, I need to rest right now." It was a lot more challenging in non-Olympic years. People were less understanding. Sometimes, being firm about the downtime I'd carved out for myself made me feel guilty, like I was letting down the people in my life. I had to remind myself of Ryan's motto and recognize that I wasn't being selfish: I was working towards my goals by resting.

It took me a long time to get here, but the word "no" has since become my best friend. It's a bit like building grit, practising saying no over and over without feeling guilty. Like any muscle, the more you use it, the stronger it grows. When I was younger, I said yes to everything. I wanted to help—to expand the game's visibility, to speak to girls' teams, to elementary schools, to any media that took the time to call. And when you don't see rest as necessary, it becomes easy to neglect.

It was most difficult to build this muscle as a parent. I'd come home from the rink exhausted, and Noah would want to go outside and play. All I wanted was to lie down on the couch and sleep. My body needed rest, but my son needed his mom.

It became a delicate balance—I could be protective of my rest time in other areas of my life, but not with Noah.

Sometimes, as a parent, you just have to perform tired. You learn to adapt. I couldn't safeguard my rest when my son needed to be at a swim meet, then a birthday party. I became more efficient. I learned to do more with less. I could no longer get an hour's rest before practice, but if I could distract Noah with some toys, I could get a 15-minute break. That was enough.

That being said, time is always in short supply, for everyone. If you are making rest a priority, it takes time away from other things. I've become an expert at prioritizing. When I was playing, my priorities were always hockey, my son, and my family—which never left much time for a social life. My circle of people remains really small. It can get a bit lonely at times, but I have the people I need. These days, my priorities have evolved to my family, my job with the Leafs, medicine, my business obligations, and my fitness. When I'm strapped for time, everything outside of these priorities gets cut. I find that I'm constantly revisiting my priorities, figuring out if a certain event or new opportunity really matters to me.

I make time for rest by literally scheduling it in my day-timer. I'm not even joking! If I don't, I won't make the time for it. My routines and rituals help. My mom always has a family dinner on Sundays. If I'm in town, I'm there every Sunday night. I like to start my day by working out at 6. I wake up knowing how my day will start, and that's one less decision that I need to make each day.

I thought I was busy as an athlete, and I actually used to give myself props for being so good at time management. But med school has taken the cake. When I first started juggling it with my Leafs job,

I felt completely tapped out. Despite having been warned, I didn't truly understand how much busier life would get in my final year.

Med school can feel like a never-ending merry-go-round of exams: you're constantly studying, you never stop writing tests. In my final year, I did eight clinical rotations—including pediatric, internal, and emergency medicine. After each rotation, I wrote an exam. That meant that after working from 9 to 5 at the hospital, I had to study for several hours every night. It felt like being stuck in a loop: I woke at dawn, worked all day, studied all night, then started all over again the next day. It was exhausting.

You can't always get a good night's sleep working in medicine. Patients need you, surgeries run long. I've pulled my fair share of night shifts and I don't love them, but it's a rite of passage for trainee doctors. I try not to sacrifice my sleep for anything, and I vividly remember pulling three midnight-to-8-a.m. shifts in a row. On the third morning, I left the hospital and drove straight to the rink for 10 a.m. practice. It hit me like a ton of bricks. It is not a feeling that I like and not a sacrifice worth making repeatedly over the long term. This stint was a short grind. It was something I had to push through, and I made time for lots of rest when the nights shifts were finally behind me.

Being bogged down with work, not knowing when—or if—the firehose I was drinking from would ever let up, was hard. The 20-hour workdays could leave me feeling hopeless. Were all the sacrifices worth it? Every truck I've owned has had a "Holy shit!" handle just above the door—the one you grab onto when things start going wrong. In that final year of med school, I felt like I was grabbing onto the holy shit handle and hanging on for dear life, wondering what was going to come at me next.

I set a really crucial intention when I first started med school: I needed to balance it. I knew there were going to be periods of time when balance wouldn't be possible and that those would be short grinds, but on the whole, I needed some hard boundaries. I watched fellow med students fall apart by focusing 100 percent on their studies. Their relationships crumbled. They gained weight. Their mental health deteriorated. It's super unhealthy. I didn't want to fall into that. I came up with a list of non-negotiables—things that I refused to give up while pursuing medicine. I had three: my family, my health, and my sleep. I was willing to walk away from med school and do something else if I felt like I had to compromise any of those three areas in the long term.

My small social circle helped. I didn't have time to keep up with everyone, so I didn't. I limited my social engagements to the bare bones. No matter what, I called my son, Noah, every day. He was 19, and it drove him crazy sometimes, but even when I was super busy, I never failed to call.

Focusing on my health and training forced me to set a limit on how much I studied. I built breaks into my schedule. Instead of sitting, I stood or paced around the back of the hall during lectures. I listened to recorded lectures while I was walking. I made sure to get my training in, even if that meant waking up a bit earlier. For one of my med school rotations, I had a 90-minute drive in each direction. On the way home every evening, I would stop midway to run for an hour in a forest grove. It was more important to me to jog in the woods than to spend that extra hour studying. When I was feeling totally spent after a long day, I would turn off my phone and my brain for a few hours. I found joy in the little things: the mornings I didn't have to wake up at 5, the nights I didn't have to study for an exam, an hour spent on my road bike (my happy place).

When I was younger, I took a lot of pride in getting excellent grades. I had an average in the high 90s from elementary through to high school. These days, if I need a 63 percent to pass, I focus on getting 63 percent so that I can pass the exam and move on. I'm not going to study one minute longer than I need to. Whether I get a 63 or a 93 percent won't change a thing in terms of how I practise medicine, so I'm not going to waste my time chasing a perfect grade. It's so much more important that I have time to train, to spend time with my loved ones, to get outdoors and do something that makes me happy. These tests are just another hoop I need to jump through.

Prioritizing rest will not always be easy. There will be times when you can't get the sleep you need, when you feel like you are clinging to the holy shit handle with everything you've got. When that happens to me, I focus on the long game. I tell myself this is just a season in my life, and that it will pass. And one day, I will look back on it and think, *Wow, that was super intense, but I made it.*

Remember, stillness is a weapon. Calmness is a weapon. So is spending time with the people you love. Like any valuable lesson, this one took me a long time to learn. I wish I had realized the value of rest when I was younger. You just can't grind it out unless you are rested.

- Rest is a weapon, not a luxury. Performance depends on it.
- Create a list of non-negotiables that you aren't willing to give up.
- Working hard doesn't mean working all the time.

4.

GET A PhD
IN EFFICIENCY

Work smarter, not harder

The winters of my childhood were long, cold, and snowy. Shaunavon, a southern Saskatchewan farming town of 1,800 hardy souls, had the same three features as most Canadian prairie towns: a church, a Chinese restaurant, and a drafty old hockey rink that sold crinkle-cut fries and the best burgers in town. In the middle of winter, it was usually colder inside that old rink than outside. Shaunavon is known in Saskatchewan for producing top-grade grains and top-level hockey players. If summers were for growing and harvesting, winter was devoted to one thing and one thing only. There wasn't much else to do other than play hockey.

Without question, the best part of my youth were Saturday nights. I spent every one of them the same way: draped over the arm of our brown corduroy easy chair, right next to Dad.

Before the sun set, we'd be settling in for a double header on *Hockey Night in Canada*.

Growing up, I wanted to be the next Wayne Gretzky or Mark Messier. I wanted to play for Edmonton, just like them. The Oilers weren't just the closest franchise to southwest Saskatchewan, they were one of the most dominant teams the NHL has ever produced. The Oil, famed for their fast-skating, exciting, offensive brand of hockey, won the Stanley Cup five times over the decade. I remember each Cup win.

"Hayley, you watch that Gretzky," Dad would say to me, tracing the hockey icon with his index finger on our little 21-inch TV screen that picked up three channels. "Look how he delays at the blue line." He'd whistle slowly as the Oilers captain rifled a pass to Paul Coffey, hitting the graceful defenceman as he came flying in late on the left side.

Dad was an educator by profession. And like the best teachers, he knew to put his students in the driver's seat. And so, before I really understood what I was doing, I was analyzing the mechanics of Messier's unique shot all on my own. I picked out the way No. 11 came gliding in on his left foot before suddenly kicking off with his right, as if he were kick-starting a temperamental motorcycle, then whipping the biscuit to the back of the net.

After watching and dissecting these skills with Dad, I'd rush outside to practise them. Maybe it was Messier's kick shot or Glenn Anderson's backhand deke. Or a toe drag. Or a top-shelf snipe. I would rush end to end like Coffey. I even wore skates several sizes too small, just like he did. I spent hours out there mimicking the game's greats. I was a student of the game long before I started pee wee.

That ended up being some of the most important learning of my career.

A lot of young players ask me what it takes to get to the top. Being born with talent helps, no question. But talent only goes so far. Whether you are innately talented or not, reaching the top of your field requires becoming a student of the game. You have to pour yourself into your passion—whether it's piano, carpentry, coding, or art—as if you were earning a PhD in it.

Becoming a master at something means working on it so much that it becomes ingrained in your DNA and you no longer have to think about it. If you practise the perfect shot from just the right angle over and over and over, eventually you can hit the target in your sleep. It takes hard work, good habits, and dedicated training—and a lot of time. As I practised on my backyard rink, the skills I was consciously, dutifully working on became automatic. When something goes from conscious to automatic, it becomes an innate part of *who you are* and how you do things. It becomes a reaction. Even when you are tired, you can still pull it out. You no longer have to think about it—you just react.

In those rare moments when you knock the puck off someone and get a clear breakaway, you have one chance to put your team up by a goal. One shot. You don't have time to think—what you do in that moment has to be automatic, a reaction. I used to study my opponents in fine detail: the way they shot, which way they turned, how they defended, when they got tired. I knew where each goalie's weaknesses lay. So, when I got that one chance, I knew what I needed to do. I just had to let my body react. I had earned a PhD in that very specific move.

It takes a lot of practice and hard work to transfer a skill, such as a quick, accurate snapshot or a toe drag, from conscious to automatic. But working hard doesn't mean working all the time. Earning a PhD in your sport is a lot like grit—both require rest, lots of it. It's a question of intensity versus volume: working smarter means finding ways to be more productive and efficient with your time rather than simply plugging away for hours on end. When I analyzed the moves I saw NHLers make on *Hockey Night in Canada*, I studied the specific things they did and worked on them until I could do them as well. Yes, I worked on them every day, but I was intentional about these efforts rather than mindlessly logging ice time.

Being more productive or working smarter doesn't require a massive shift in how you approach your work. For me, it meant being more systematic and methodical with my time. It meant being better organized and sticking to the schedules I set for myself. It was about making the most of my time rather than working all. the. time. How can you find efficiencies that allow you to squeeze more out of every hour and every day? To stay alert and on task, I like to work in focused, short bursts. I have a routine and don't deviate from it. I stick to my schedule even when it comes to taking breaks. On my best days, I use social media as a communications tool, not as a time waster.

I have always consulted experts in order to sharpen my game. I read a ton of biographies of great leaders from business, sports, and history. I watched documentaries about high achievers in medicine, sciences, and the arts. I sought out experts, like development coach Darryl Belfry. Darryl, who has been labelled the "superstar whisperer," has a client list that includes Sidney Crosby, Patrick Kane, Nathan MacKinnon, and Jonathan Toews. He helped me reinvent my game for the last ten years of my career.

Before he started working with me, Darryl created an analytical profile of my game, breaking it down shift by shift. He knew more about how I played than I did—when, where, and how I tended to touch the puck and to what effect. He knew what adjustments I needed to make to improve my production. He used video footage from my games to explain that I was taking 60 percent of my shots from a certain area of the ice but was scoring on less than 2 percent of them. These he called wasted shots. He was right. I stopped that real quick. He showed me precisely what I needed to do to increase my numbers and production.

Three times a year, I flew down to Naples, Florida, where he lives, to train at the Florida Everblades facility in Fort Myers for four or five days at a time. Ahead of the 2014 Sochi Winter Olympic Games, we did a deep dive on each of Team USA's players, studying every aspect of their games—how they turned, where they tended to pass, what their weaknesses were. Darryl put together video for myself and my linemates, Meghan Agosta and Natalie Spooner. I have no doubt that was the reason we were the most consistent line at that Olympics.

Film helped me work smarter and make the most of my time. A lot of kids today tell me they don't watch hockey like I did with Dad back in the day (and still do now). But I strongly believe that to become the best, you have to learn from the best. I have always been a visual learner. Long before my coaches were recording our games, I studied whatever video I could get my hands on. I had Don Cherry's *Rock'em Sock'em* collection and recordings of classic Stanley Cup finals. I figured out how to order tapes of the '72 Summit Series, the eight-game matchup between the USSR and Canada, and bought footage of the old Russian Red Army team practices.

I find that once I see something, I am able to replicate it. The vision seems to imprint into my brain, almost like a video I can then replay on the ice. After I saw tapes of Gretzky delaying at the blue line, I could close my eyes and walk through the play. When I lay in bed, it was like watching a movie—I would run through each play. When I hit the ice, I was able to recreate the move, the play.

Studying video trained me to become hyperaware of the ice surrounding me, to pick up on the nuances and subtleties that I might otherwise have missed. I find that this practice also helps me in medicine. It allows me to quickly read non-verbal cues that my patients are signalling: their tensions, fears, hesitation.

Visualization was another major part of my regimen, and it became more deliberate and sophisticated as I grew older. Before big games, I would lie in my hotel room tracing a serpentine path for myself through the offensive end in my mind's eye. I would tense my core as I faked left. I could almost smell the pungent mixture of freshly laundered jerseys, sweat, and popcorn in the rink. I truly believe that we can manifest things that we never saw as possible by walking through them in our minds this way first. Just like telling your body it isn't tired in order to push through, your brain doesn't differentiate between the images that you are visualizing and the scenes that you are really seeing in front of you. That is why visualization can be so effective. It's smart work.

—

Getting a PhD in efficiency doesn't mean becoming an expert in every aspect of your sport or profession. That's unreasonable and ineffective. When I was playing, I focused on offence. I knew what my responsibilities were in the defensive zone, but I didn't focus on what was required of goalies and defencemen. I put my energy where my strengths lay: in attacking and shooting. And I worked on those areas until they were reactions. No one can be good at everything; I had to prioritize what I wanted to work on. I keyed in on specific aspects I needed to excel at and let the rest of it slide, which allowed me to budget my time and make room for rest.

In business, I focus on the one or two things I need to know in order to help my companies thrive. Because I have spent so much time giving speeches and doing media interviews, I can prepare very quickly to speak to media or investors. I don't have to worry over what I'm going to say or study my key messaging. I've done it so many times that it's become a habit, something I do easily and well. I'm not naturally an outgoing person, but I have honed that skill by watching other people speak and giving talks to the mirror over and over again. Over the years, it has become second nature to me. Now, my prep time for an interview is next to nil. Similarly I don't allow myself to get caught up in the smaller minutiae of my companies—learning how to run the accounting or payroll software. That's not a good use of my time and I'm really not very good at it. I don't need to sit in on every meeting. I focus instead on the high-level budgets, public relations, and sponsor outreach—that's my wheelhouse. Where it might take my staff several days and multiple emails and phone calls to get an invite to a figure skater like Tessa Virtue or a soccer player like Christine Sinclair, I can text them and have an answer in seven seconds. I am careful to hire people smarter than me who have expertise that I don't, and I trust them to do the work—the same way I trusted the defence to protect our zone. I empower them to do the job I hired them to do, and then I get the hell out of the way and let them do it.

You can maximize the intensity and minimize the volume of your work all you want—but earning a PhD in your passion will still take years of dedication. The more something becomes a habit or a reflex, the easier it becomes and the more fun you can have with it. Becoming the best is also about how you talk to yourself, how you sleep, how you eat, who you choose to surround yourself with, how you engage with others, how you choose to expend your energy. It's also about learning from the best, gathering intel and methods, not recreating the wheel. To me, it has less to do with physical work than with mental fortitude. This may sound a bit neurotic and over the top, but if you think about it, every single moment of the day we are making decisions. It's about making consistent decisions—each one bringing you one step closer to your dreams.

And passion is what seeds those dreams. I couldn't have grinded it out for all those years if I hadn't loved what I was doing. I would have burned out, got injured, or become a jerk to the people I love. My PhD started on my backyard rink for a reason. I loved the *thwaaaack* of the puck against the homemade plywood boards and the *ksssh-ksssh-ksssh* as my blades cut into the ice. Best of all, I loved that nobody could bug me. There were no moms glaring at me. No bullies to run me down. No one could touch me there. It was my safe place. I never felt more alive than I did on that little rink.

The work never once felt forced. It never felt like an obligation. I loved the game with all my heart, and I was willing to do whatever it took to become the best.

- Whether you are innately talented or not, reaching the top requires becoming a student of your field.

- High volume of ill-defined practice isn't as effective as shorter bursts of intensely focused practice.

- To become the best, you have learn from the best. Read the best. Watch the best.

5.

COMPETE EACH DAY

Small habits = big success

My friends in medicine like to tease me about my fixation on always being early. It isn't just me. It's something most athletes have in common. When I was 22 years old, I met Martin Gélinas. I was newly returned from Salt Lake, following my first gold medal triumph over the U.S. Martin was brand new to Calgary, having just signed with the Flames as an unrestricted free agent.

The day we met, I was speaking to his team at the Saddledome, Calgary's home barn. Martin sought me out afterwards. I think he could sense that my intensity and drive were a close match to his own. Either that or he just didn't know too many folks in the city and needed some new friends!

"We should train together," Martin said by way of introduction. I was well aware of his speed, work ethic, and conditioning; in hockey circles, they are legendary. The average career length for an NHLer is five years. Martin was entering his 17th year in the league. He didn't show any sign of slowing down, and I wanted to push my training to a higher level. Pairing up made perfect sense.

I told him to meet me at the gym the next morning at 7:30. I got there a little early to greet him. I needn't have bothered. Marty had been waiting for me to arrive since 7 a.m., running on a treadmill.

The next day, I figured I'd beat him. But when I arrived at 6:30 a.m., Marty was already warming up, a big, goofy grin on his face.

I managed to clock in first the next day by showing up at 6:15 a.m. The day after that, Marty was waiting for me when I came at 6 a.m., chuckling over my crestfallen face. It became a long-running game between us: who would get to training first. That's the thing about athletes: everything is a competition.

Our contest of who-can-be-the-earliest-bird may come off as silly, but I've found that it's the tiny, seemingly insignificant habits that make all the difference in the long run. Success lies in the details. Crisp passes, proper power-lifting form, never cheating on a sprint—doing these things properly gives you tiny, marginal gains. It makes you just a little bit better each day. And executing these small habits consistently, day in, day out, is how the big successes happen. How you complete the little things says a lot about you as a person. The shape of the report you turn in at work, how you arrive at a meeting, the tone you use on the phone—all of these aspects communicate what you consider to be important. If you take pride in your work, you don't turn in a report with typos in it. If you are invested in landing a client, you aren't flippant in your conversations with them. Showing up late doesn't mean that you are carefree and fun; it shows that you didn't care enough about the meeting to be on time. These little things are all signs of diligence (or lack thereof).

One of the first things I noticed in medical school was that athletes tended to be the ones who showed up on time. In sports, being punctual is a given. Practices, lifts, games, buses, they wait for no one. If you are late, you miss out and the team as a whole suffers. In my classes, there were a few of us athletes who showed up early for every 8:30 a.m. lecture. Most were former football or basketball players—guys who played in the CFL or at the varsity level in university. And me.

A lot of my classmates were still pulling out their laptops and wrestling with their bags and coats for several minutes after the lecture began. Some would walk in five minutes into the lecture, opening the classroom door, walking up the stairs right in front of the professor, looking flustered and anxious—not a great state of mind in which to absorb an epidemiology lecture. In contrast, the group of us already there were settled in: busy taking notes, absorbing the information, feeling relaxed. We had set ourselves up for success by being early and ready to learn. When you execute well on the little things, you're setting yourself up for bigger and better things.

This stuff is boring as Bob, I know that. It's obvious, but the truth is, most of us don't do the obvious. We all know what we *should* be doing. The trick is going out there and actually doing it. And committing to doing the boring stuff in order to win each day. None of this is rocket science: it's just building the habits you need to set yourself up for success. There's an old story about J.P. Morgan that I love; he was an American banker and financier who dominated Wall Street in the decades before the First World War. Morgan was once shown an envelope said to contain a "guaranteed formula for success." He agreed that if he found the advice written inside useful, he would pay $25,000 for it. Morgan opened the envelope, nodded, and paid up.

There were two steps to the formula:

1. *Every morning, write a list of the things that need to be done that day.*
2. *Do them.*

Not exactly groundbreaking. But I love to-do lists. They are beautiful in their simplicity. Every day, you figure out what needs to be done and in what order; you write down the tasks; and then, one by one, you knock off the items on your list. You break larger goals down into manageable pieces. You find a way to win each day.

Big journeys are daunting, whether it's to a new job, a new degree program, or an Olympic final. Something that large is overwhelming to process. Or it may not be just "one" thing—life tends to compound. We have professional responsibilities, family responsibilities, other goals we are chasing. But big goals don't just happen. They are the result of a million small, smart choices. If you break things down into small pieces and keep chipping away, anything can become manageable.

I've found myself living a professional life that requires a ton of travel and conflicting obligations. I have exams to study for, reports and training programs due to the Leafs, and speaking obligations that take me all over North America. And I decided to write a book in the middle of it all. It's stressful and overwhelming—I needed a plan to manage life and my anxiety. In creating a plan, I was taking back some control.

I seem to have found myself in a very similar situation to that of a mentor of mine, Peter Jensen, the longtime sports psychologist with the national women's hockey team. Peter is also a performance coach, author, and motivational speaker with a jam-packed schedule. He always seems to be headed to the airport to catch a plane. Years ago, I asked him how he managed to travel so much and handle his overwhelming schedule so well.

"Sure, I'm travelling a lot," he said. "But today, I'm going from Toronto to Winnipeg. That's what I'm doing today. I'm not going Toronto-Winnipeg-Frankfurt-London-Seattle-Calgary. That's my two-week schedule. Today, I'm only going to Winnipeg. So that's what I'm going to focus on." He continued, breaking down his big-picture obligations into manageable pieces: "When I get to the city, I'm going to go to the hotel. I'm going to lie down and take a 30-minute nap. When I wake up, I'm going to shower and prepare for the speech I'm giving."

Peter's approach really resonated with me and helped me come up with my own strategy to managing stress and staying organized. I tend to focus on the work or travel that I need to do on a given day, and not let myself stress out about the exams and engagements piling up behind it. I focus like a hawk on the day's plan, on the next action item on my daily list. The rest can wait.

Sometimes, taking it day by day isn't enough and I'll divide my days into a series of what I like to call "micro-chunks," periods of a couple hours each. This way, I can't get too far ahead of myself. Micro-chunking my days makes my schedule simple and straightforward. It helps me avoid becoming paralyzed by anxiety. Micro-productivity helps me to reduce stress and fatigue and stay focused and calm. It allows me to work backwards from a long-term goal and win each day.

While studying medicine, I learned why the strategy is so effective. By breaking down the larger, big-ticket goals into smaller, actionable items, I was setting myself up for a series of small wins each day. Every short-term win creates its own momentum. It feels good to get a win, even a tiny one! With it comes a little burst of satisfaction, and the motivation to keep going, to check off another item on my to-do list.

The rush of accomplishment I feel every time I scratch off a task from my to-do list is the result of the release of dopamine. The neurotransmitter works by making us feel joyful, animated, lighthearted, and good. Those are great feelings! Our brains link these feelings with ticking off a chore from our to-do list, so we want to keep doing them. Neurobiologically, the satisfaction of completing a task energizes us to keep going, to keep doing the thing that made us feel that way. This is how good habits are formed. The more items you check off your to-do list, the more likely you are to keep moving down it, because you're leap-frogging from one success to the next. What I am doing is turning a marathon into a series of short sprints.

For me, the hardest thing is always getting started. Once I take the first step, I begin building momentum. By accomplishing small, manageable tasks on the daily, I'm also building confidence in myself. What starts off feeling like a daunting, impossible task—like writing a book!—will begin to feel more achievable once you get going.

When I'm micro-chunking my day, I always draw up a list. It helps ease my anxiety: once I map it out on paper, it feels less daunting. Yes, I'm very analog—I still use a paper diary. In med school, the other students were constantly making fun of me. I was one of the only students in our class who didn't use a laptop or an iPad to take notes. It may be old school, but the research shows that by physically jotting things down, you tend to retain them better than if you type them. People love their gadgets, but in my book, paper trumps tech any day of the week.

I keep my paper lists, as the log of previous days helps me down the road. When I was still training with the national team, I would fill up logbooks with every single training session. In my garage, I have boxes filled with logbooks going back 20 years. I could look up exactly what training I completed on, say, August 12, 2002: how fast I was running, how much I was lifting, how many hours I logged on the ice that day, and what my resting heart rate was when I cooled down.

Tracking your workouts helps you spot trends. It can help you understand why your fatigue levels are decreasing, for example, or why you are putting on muscle. If you don't write it all down, it's easy to lose that valuable data. I can't tell you how many times the small, seemingly insignificant step of logging a workout has helped me down the line when I needed to go back and look something up. It's a tiny habit that has paid off in spades.

Paying attention to these small choices doesn't have to be boring. On Team Canada, we built a culture of diligence in details with a focus on fun. This philosophy kept us from tuning out the small details when they became too tedious, and it was key to our success.

In the middle of the national team dressing room at WinSport in Calgary, there is a huge Team Canada logo. Whenever we travelled for games, we brought a fancy carpet with the logo printed onto it. The carpet would always be placed at the centre of the visitors' dressing room, a place of pride. As many hockey teams do, we considered the logo sacred. Nothing could be placed on it, not a laundry cart, not a skate, not a towel. You couldn't walk across it. If a teammate accidentally stepped on it, there was trouble.

If someone touched the logo, they had to pay a fine. But simply putting money in a jar is too easy. Becky Kellar, that amazing competitor who moved herself and her kids to Calgary to centralize every fourth year, has a wicked sense of humour. She made up a fine-paying ceremony: she'd put on a mouldy old jockstrap with an empty Gatorade bottle taped to it, and the person who'd mistakenly stepped on the logo would have to try to toss a Double Bubble gum into the bottle. While Becky was dancing. If she missed, she had to pay a $2 fine.

We would stand in a circle around Becky and her opponent, chanting: "Pay your fine! Pay your fine!" Becky would be half-dressed, wearing this ridiculous cup, swaying her hips back and forth to make it more difficult to hit the target. Everyone would end up doubled over laughing. Executing the details doesn't have to be tedious.

As a culture, we have become fixated on chasing the quick fix, the life hack we hope will deliver top results with minimal effort. There is a reason these things are so elusive. There are no shortcuts to success. The small things, done consistently, add up in the long run. If you cut corners, you will never see the results you are chasing.

When I wake up every morning, I have one goal (in true athlete form): I want to win each day. That means I want to win my arrival at the rink by arriving early and being relaxed. I want to win the warm-up at practice by paying attention to the details. I want to win my list of obligations by writing them down so I don't forget something important. I'm not competing against anyone else—I'm trying to beat myself and what I did the day before. Believe me, a gold medal isn't a single-game prospect; it's a four-year grind.

- Attention to the little things says a lot about who we are and who we strive to be.

- Turn a marathon into a series of short sprints.

- Small habits and choices, done consistently, add up in the long run.

THE NEUTRAL ZONE

Get creative

IN HOCKEY, ONCE YOU HIT your blue line, the pressure starts to lift. With your net 70 feet behind you, the risk of being scored on drops. You are no longer defending and preventing goals. You can let go of the regimented systems that got you out of the defensive zone. You can inject a little creativity into your game.

While your priorities are clear in the D zone, the neutral zone can feel a bit like a no man's land. It is the space in between. Sometimes, you'll skate straight up the ice and hit the offensive zone flying. Other times your path will be blocked, and you'll need to go east-west before advancing down ice. When all else fails, the best plan is circling back into your end to start over, going backwards in order to go forward.

The defensive zone is all about systems and building a foundation, the habits you rely on to avoid getting scored on. The neutral zone is where you fine-tune your approach, where you transition from defending to scoring. It takes imagination and inventiveness. To keep growing and evolving, both as a player and a person, I have become a seeker in everything that I do.

A lot goes into this in-between area, this undefined section that gets me from point A to point B. It's easy to get lost and start questioning what the hell I'm doing. That's why it's so crucial to build joy and play into my day-to-day life.

When you hit a rough patch in life, it can feel like you're stuck in the neutral zone, trying to break through. You try to muscle past the defender only to get turned around; your teammate tries chipping the puck off the boards but it gets knocked back at you; the other team decides to run a neutral zone trap, halting *everything*. It can be frustrating, infuriating. But you can't get to the net without first clearing the neutral zone.

6.

BE A SEEKER

You can't grow by standing still

Coming out of the 2002 Salt Lake Games, I wanted to give my game a new look. By that point, I had played in two Olympics and four World Championships. We were the best women's hockey team in the world. I was 24 and had realized many of my hockey dreams. That scared the shit out of me.

A lot of people spend their entire lives chasing their goals—it gives them purpose, drive, motivation every day. Something to work towards. What you don't hear about is what happens *after*. Once you've realized your dreams, then what? I was one of the game's best female players. I didn't feel challenged by my club team anymore and I was afraid of stagnating. How would I keep growing if I didn't feel challenged when I went to the rink? Was this it for me? Was this as far as I could go?

Between Olympic years, I'd been playing at the highest level for women in Canada, the original National Women's Hockey League (a senior women's league). It was amateur—we weren't being paid at all and in fact had to pay for our ice time—but it was where all the top players in Canada were. By 2002, I'd been there for almost a decade and the level of competition felt easy to me. My club team was where I spent the majority of my time practising and playing between Olympics. But we practised only a couple times a week and we didn't play as many games in a season as I would have liked. I wanted to experience life as a professional hockey player, day in and day out, not only in Olympic years.

It didn't take long to realize that I needed a creative solution. As an athlete, I was constantly assessing and reassessing the way I did things. I tracked the game's best players, both on the men's and women's sides. I studied how they played and how they trained. I saw what the next level up in hockey looked like for me, and I knew that I wouldn't find it in the women's game in North America. I needed to find an opportunity for myself.

At the same time as this restlessness set in, I was thinking about changing up my style of play. I wanted to rely less on my physical game and become more of a finesse player. I wanted to be less predictable. In my seven years with the Canadian national team, I had developed a power-focused style of play: I was bigger, stronger, and faster than my opponents and had been using my physicality to bend the game to my will, running over and shoving players off the puck. I played like a bull. Though that style had been working for me, I didn't want to depend on it alone. I wanted to be versatile. When you play one team as many times as we do the Americans, you get to know a player's habits, their weaknesses, the holes in their game. Team USA knew me inside and out by that point, and the next time we met, I wanted to surprise them. Instead of always being a bull, I wanted to become what Darryl Belfry calls a "spider."

When you're a spider, the puck comes to you and through you. You don't need to haul the biscuit around the ice; it's following *you* around the rink. You're constantly engaging with it. You're finding seams, getting open, one-timing the puck to a winger in order to immediately get it back again. You're cycling in and out of the play. Rather than playing by force, you are forcing the play. Rather than doing it all yourself, you are creating opportunities for your team. If I built out my game so that I could be the bull or the spider, or something in between, the Americans would always be on their back foot trying to figure me out.

I also wanted to get back to the mentality of being a rookie, being a seeker. Being the new one on the team requires a growth mindset; it's challenging, exciting, and a huge learning curve. It's not just about literally being the new person: it's a way of thinking where you're constantly looking for new ways to improve. I've found that unless I'm taking chances and pushing the envelope, I get antsy. I start to feel like I'm not really living, like I'm moving backwards. It spreads to other areas of my life, and I get grumpy and short-tempered. It's not good for me—or the people who have to live with me! I'm restless when I feel my growth slowing down, when I am no longer learning something new every day. When I'm growing, I'm off-centre, unsure, playing catch-up—in a good way. I wanted to stop feeling comfortable, to be that rookie again who is asking questions and finding new approaches to my training and my game. I wanted to get back to being a seeker.

So, in the fall of 2002, I set out to find somewhere to play men's pro hockey.

My likeliest bet for a good fit was a league in Europe. It wasn't the easiest decision I've ever made; I worried about leaving Canada and my family. Noah wasn't yet four, and I dreaded being away from him and the rest of my support system. I knew there would be anger and jealousy from some of my teammates and others in the women's game who wouldn't appreciate what I was doing. I knew I would be lambasted in the media. But larger than any of those downsides was my fear that if I just kept doing what I was doing, I would never get to see my potential through to the end. When I asked myself what I wanted to achieve, the answer was simple: I wanted to become the best hockey player that I could be. And I was willing to do whatever it took to achieve that. I knew I could play in a men's pro league; I didn't have any doubts that I wasn't good enough. For the previous two summers I had spent time in the Czech Republic, practising and training with HC Energie Karlovy Vary, a top-tier team. It was only for a couple of months at a time, but it had shown me that I could compete with those players at that level. Now I wanted to do it for an entire season.

Initially, I had my heart set on playing the 2003 season in Italy. I had a great contract lined up with the Merano Eagles and was just a signature away from earning a solid salary as an import player. That would have been huge for me; aside from some card-ing money from Team Canada, I had never been paid to play before. But this plan stopped at the paperwork stage: the Italian Ice Hockey Federation refused to register me. They said that women could play on a men's team only if no parallel women's league existed. Because there were senior women's leagues in Canada, they considered those parallel and argued that I should stay there. The league president was more direct with Canadian media, telling the CBC that he felt the whole thing was a publicity stunt.

I was disappointed. So was Merano's coach, Paul Theriault, a Canadian from Sault Ste. Marie who was familiar with my game. Theriault knew I had the talent to play in that league, and he had a role carved out for me with the Eagles. The team's management was prepared to challenge the federation's ruling on my behalf, but I knew it was a lost cause. The powers-that-be were dead set against me playing in Italy, and I knew they weren't going to reverse course. I told the Eagles not to bother appealing the decision and I kept searching for a team and league that wanted me.

A German team expressed interest in me, but the league didn't feel like the right fit. NHL legend Phil Esposito approached my agent with an offer for a 15-game tryout with the Cincinnati Cyclones of the East Coast Hockey League (ECHL). Today, the ECHL is a solid NHL feeder league. But 20 years ago, it had a reputation for being a goon league. I wasn't interested in that style of play and didn't think it would advance my goal of becoming a spider. I imagined everyone in that league would focus on running me over. If I wanted to become more versatile, I needed to be around skills-focused players.

I joined HC Salamat in Suomi-sarja, Finland's third division, centring the team's third line. Moving to suburban Kirkko-nummi, outside of Helsinki, was a huge culture shock, which was heightened by moving there solo. Noah was able to come to Finland a few times with our nanny, Janice, and my sister, Jane. But mostly I was alone in a small town on the Baltic Sea, surrounded by people who spoke a different language from me and ate things I'd never heard of before—cabbage rolls and pickled herring and fish pies!

Winters in Finland can be rough. I was living north of the 60th parallel, about the same latitude as Anchorage, Alaska. When I left for the gym in the morning, it was dark. I'd go to the rink in the afternoon and it would be dark. I'd come out of the rink in the evening and it would be dark. The skies were a decent match for my mood.

I was attracting a fair bit of attention. Media was even showing up for Salamat practices. But head coach Matti Hagman, who had played for the Edmonton Oilers in the late '70s, didn't exactly roll out the welcome mat for me. At my first practice, he assigned a six-foot-four defenceman to hound me and take runs at me. Every time he drilled me, I picked myself up off the ice and moved on to the next drill, knowing it would happen again and again all practice long. What else could I do? He never let up. After two weeks, Matti finally called him off. "I had to do that," he told me. "I wanted the media to see you could handle the hitting."

A lot of people thought my move to Finland was a publicity stunt. It was frustrating. I stood to gain nothing from a bit of extra press. It wasn't like sponsors were falling all over themselves to sign female hockey players in 2003. (Or today, for that matter.) My choice had nothing to do with media attention or breaking barriers. I was there to take my game to the next level. It was a hard thing for people on the outside to understand.

I couldn't have chosen a more dramatic situation to force me to stop playing like a bull. I was suddenly one of the smaller players on the ice. I couldn't run over opponents anymore—most of them were bigger and stronger than me. I wasn't able to use pure power to get the puck. The switch to full-contact hockey also forced me to change how I saw the ice; I needed to play with eyes in the back of my head, especially as a centre coming up the middle. Full contact means you can't just follow the puck, you have to always know what is coming at you. One bad hit could end my career.

I was forced to become a spider. I still went hard into the corners. I threw checks. I played tough, but I started relying more on my intelligence than my brute strength, replacing slapshots with quicker, smart shots and executing creative passes. The bull was slowly disappearing.

I finished the season with Salamat's best faceoff numbers and became the first woman to score in men's pro, with two goals and 10 assists over 23 games. Even better, Salamat moved up to Finland's second division. After returning to Canada in between, I played a further 17 games with the team the following season, logging seven more goals and six assists.

When I got back to Alberta, I decided to surprise Noah. My flight got in around midnight. I kneeled down beside his bed and rubbed his back until he woke up. "Mommy, you're home!" he said, grabbing me in a tight hug. He didn't stop talking for the next two hours. He needed to catch me up on everything he was learning about dinosaurs and the latest daycare gossip.

The experience was tough on me and my family. But nothing could have been better for my game. When I rejoined my old team in Calgary, I was able to read the ice much more quickly. I had so much more time and space. I brought a new patience and poise to my game. There had been a lot of dark, lonely days, but it was worth it. Those two seasons in Finland were two of the best of my hockey career.

You grow by taking chances. You reach your dreams by challenging yourself. When I look back at 2002 now, I see that I had two clear choices: I could stay where I was comfortable, or I could seek out an entirely new challenge and find out who I could become. Nothing about it was easy, but it was one of the best decisions I ever made.

Being a seeker is a mindset, one that forces you to grow. I never settled for safe. I never did what had been done before. If I was getting sick of the gym, I got outside. If I was getting bored or complacent, I changed things up. And I never trained with my equals, not if I could help it. I worked out with people who were bigger, stronger, or faster, or who had something new to teach me. It's the best way to improve. It forces you to work harder and think faster because you're always chasing them, you're always playing catch-up.

When I was younger, I trained with dogged, hardworking NHLers like Martin Gélinas and Andrew Ference in the off-season. Andrew was a lower-drafted player, but he went on to log more than 900 games in the NHL. His diligence and preparation lit a fire in me. I have never been short on drive or focus in the gym, but man, I had to dig deep just to keep up with Andrew and Martin. Training with them helped deepen my tolerance for pain. Martin's commitment and intensity were inspiring, especially how hard he worked to become faster and stronger in the twilight of his career. Years later, when I was fighting my own battle against Father Time, I would think often of Martin, and what he was able to achieve in the last six years of his career.

Those summers I had spent in the Czech Republic were a lot more than just ice time with HC Energie Karlovy Vary. I was also training with a retired Soviet army sergeant, Stanislav Nevesly. He had a wicked sense of humour and ground me into the dirt. Every. single. day. He had a classic Soviet training mentality and spoke in a bark, running me through a mixture of strength-based and explosive aerobic routines that included gymnastics, kettle balls, tennis, and sprinting through the forest as though I was being chased. And this was in the afternoons. I spent the mornings on the ice with the Energie. In Europe, pro hockey seasons start earlier than they do in North America. A lot of teams will train together all summer. In the NHL, when the season is over, most players head back to their hometowns and report for training camp in the fall. The Energie started their training camp in early July and welcomed me to join them as they prepared for the season.

Every evening, I would limp to my car, exhausted, soaked in sweat. I loved every minute of my time with Stanislav. This is what I lived for. I think that's why I played as long as I did. These vastly different ways of training were so new, exciting, exhilarating. Being challenged and putting myself in an underdog position every day, and then getting through those challenges, made me feel invincible. There was nothing I couldn't conquer, no challenge I couldn't take on.

I branched out even further as my career continued, searching for even more varied ways to get stronger and improve. I moved from hockey-specific trainers to hiring Kelsey Andries, a six-foot-tall, tattooed Muay Thai fighter and trainer, to run programs for me. Kelsey, who has since become a good friend, is a former hockey player and freestyle wrestler. She had me working out with athletes from other sports—track athletes from the local university, speed skaters, and Olympic bobsledders, like Kaillie Humphries. This was an entirely new challenge. Each of us brought our unique strengths to the table. For me, it was speed and agility. The bobsledders brought explosive power and strength. The sprinters were elastic and fast. The cross-country skiers had unbelievable cardiovascular fitness. Competing with them around the track or gym meant pushing my fitness level to new heights. I loved it.

In the late 2000s and 2010s, I (along with the rest of the world!) was entranced by the speed that had entered the NHL. Sidney Crosby and Nathan MacKinnon could shift into entirely different gears on the ice. I sought out their trainer, Andy O'Brien, to see if I could increase my own game speed. After analyzing my stride and movement patterns on one smoking-hot day in Florida, Andy told me that I wasn't moving as efficiently as I needed to be.

He broke down the biomechanics of movement for me. He got me doing track-based workouts, focusing on speed development. He helped me make gains in agility, critical power, and speed endurance—the ability to find another, higher gear.

The curiosity inherent in being a seeker often leads you to find weaknesses you wouldn't have otherwise. While I was working on my speed with Andy, I realized that I needed to become more flexible. Hockey players are typically pretty stiff and rigid. We get tight shoulders, groins, and hips. Being too tight is a great way to get hurt. I sought out Syl Corbett, a Calgary-based professional mountain runner, physiologist, and trainer with a PhD in neuro-physiology. The first day she worked on me, Syl burst out laughing. "Oh my god, you are such a project." Syl introduced me to a combination of stretches to help increase my range of motion and neural activation so that I could fire up the right muscles ahead of games and workouts.

I did a lot of work to open up my hips, to make them more dynamic and increase their range of motion. That's how you become more powerful and fluid. That's also how you extend your longevity in the game. Working on flexibility can be super frustrating, though. You're not adding to your biceps or vertical leap. The benefits aren't immediately evident. The work can be tedious. And it's hard to maintain your flexibility while you're also trying to build muscle mass.

There was another reason I was doing it: when your body's tight, your mind is, too. If I get too narrow in my thinking, I don't move well either. I don't flow. In opening up my body, I was trying to open up my mind. I'm a pretty driven, intense person. Staying loose and free allows me to be more creative in life and on the ice.

I'm no longer playing hockey, but I'm still working on my fitness and flexibility. It helps me stay loose and relaxed through long shifts in the ER or a hospital ward, where I can spend 14 hours on my feet. And, of course, I'm still a seeker. These days, it's my mentors in medicine and my professors that I'm peppering with questions.

It always surprises me how many med students are afraid of looking "stupid." It's as if they don't want to reveal that they are simply a rookie, someone who is still learning. I'm very comfortable putting up my hand and giving the wrong answer. Lord knows

I've done it time and time again! Perhaps it's because I'm in my early 40s, not in my 20s like many of my classmates, that I'm not afraid to look silly in front of people. Though come to think of it, I've never been afraid of looking silly or asking dumb questions. I'm good with it. To me, trying is the only way forward. If I worried about looking dumb, I would miss out on opportunities to improve. Right now, I probably look out of my league about 5,789 times a day. I know that getting an answer wrong is not a reflection of who I am, but of what I'm learning. As long as I keep failing forward, I know I'm on the right track.

When you're on the outside of medicine looking in, you probably think doctors have all the answers. Now that I am inside the profession, I realize that I don't know everything. Sometimes it feels like I don't really know anything at all. The more I learn, the more I realize how little I know. It's humbling. It also makes me hungry to learn more. I'm pretty sure I will feel that way throughout my entire medical career. The doctors who are able to admit when they don't know something are the ones that I feel safest around. They know their limitations. It's the other guys I worry about.

When a supervising physician asks me if I can put in a central line, I reply honestly but show an eagerness to learn: "I haven't done it yet, but I'm totally willing to try if you're going to show me." You can't learn hands-on skills like these in a lecture theatre. Inside, I might be thinking, *Oh my god, I should not be doing this*, but knowing that I'm standing beside a woman who's done 10,000 of them helps set my mind at ease.

I could talk for days about all the mistakes I have made as a med student. On many occasions, my supervising doctors have called me out for doing something incorrectly, sometimes in front of fellow colleagues or even patients. One doc wasn't too impressed with how I'd presented a patient case. In front of my peers, he told me that my presentation was crap and that I needed to provide more pertinent information and drop the unimportant stuff.

At that point, some trainees might have thought to themselves, *Oh no. He thinks I'm a bad student.* Or, *I'm bad at what I'm doing. I'm never going to be a doctor.* Getting comfortable with being corrected is all part of the seeker mentality. You need people to give you feedback, even if it doesn't feel good at the time. During my hockey career, I was told that I was doing something wrong or that I needed to be better almost daily. I got used to having my performance evaluated, day in, day out.

When my supervising doctor called me out that day, I thought to myself, *Oh man, I am on the struggle bus big time right now!* It was shitty but it was also great, because he was telling me where I was falling short. Being told all the things you do incorrectly can *feel* like failure. But it's not. It's how you course correct. The way I see it, that doctor was also telling me that he believes I might actually have some potential. Otherwise, he probably wouldn't bother telling me what to improve on.

Embrace the suck, enjoy the struggle bus! Mistakes, failures— don't shy away from them. Don't get hung up on them. Don't get embarrassed by them. It's rarely personal. People are too busy worrying about themselves to spend time worrying about you.

There are a lot of reasons why people shy away from throwing themselves into unfamiliar situations. Being a rookie is difficult and isolating. When you're trying something new and finding ways to improve, it's uncomfortable. It can be brutal, in fact.

When I was 10, I begged my parents to let me go to the Valley Hockey School, an elite summer camp run out of the Regina Agridome. All the best kids my age from southern Saskatchewan went to it. It was run by Lorne Davis, who scouted for the Oilers. Lorne let me register for camp, but he didn't have a place for me to sleep. All the boys slept in a dorm at a nearby university.

I was desperate to skate at this camp and refused to be deterred. Eventually, camp organizers found a place for me: a closet down the hall from the boys' dorm. I brought a sleeping bag and pillow from home with me. Every night, I hunkered down between a couple of brooms and a bucket. Above me, a bunch of dusty old coats hung from a closet rod.

I hated being singled out that way. I just wanted to be treated like a hockey player, like everyone else. But I was willing to do whatever it took to elevate my game.

When I first arrived in Finland, my discomfort was constant and intense. I didn't have many friends; I didn't speak the language. I felt isolated and lonely as hell, like an outsider who didn't belong. It took a few months to get comfortable and get to know people, many of whom remain amazing friends to this day.

My team ended up being a saving grace. That first season, one of our assistant coaches would pop into my dressing room before games: "Okay, Hayley, number 11 and number 67, they're going to try to take you out today." This allowed me to prepare for it. I was mentally aware of what was coming. I would look at the bench next door and keep my eyes on the players in question. When I was on a shift with one of them, I always knew where they were on the ice.

I wore a visor instead of the full cage we wear in the women's game. I never thought I would miss my cage until I took an Easton Synergy stick across the bridge of my nose in one of my first games with Salamat. The crack was so loud even the fans heard it. Blood gushed from my nose like it was a fountain. When I got to the bench, the guys were horrified. I grabbed the door with two hands and slammed it as hard as I could. I had been run at during every game and every practice in front of the media for weeks on end leading up to that moment. It just plain sucked. I was so incredibly uncomfortable with everything I had chosen for that season, and this was a breaking point, literally.

I grabbed my nose and shifted it back into place. I decided to try out my Finnish. "*Pikku!*" I shouted, and sat down. I thought I'd said "Fuck."

One of my teammates, Immo—the team's tough guy who became a close friend—handed me a towel, and I put it over my face. "Hayley, it's *vittu*," he said. We both laughed—turns out the "swear word" I yelled actually means "small child." Then I buried my tears of frustration in the towel. Dealing with all the other crap I was dealing with hurt more than the broken nose. But I didn't want the guys or the media to see me cry.

For a week I had a pair of black eyes, and I still have a bump on the bridge of my nose—my souvenir from Finland. A couple nights later I got my first goal, a backhand, in front of a sellout crowd of 1,200 at our home rink. I forgot all about my sore nose. I had reached one of my goals—the pursuit of which had put me so far out of my comfort zone in the first place—I was improving my game.

When we played our rival, the Savonlinnan Pallokerho, or SaPKo, their head coach told reporters that he'd brought up a pair of goons to knock the daylights out of me. That, I was okay with. What infuriated me was where SaPKo had me change before the game. Instead of opening up a dressing room for me, they stuck me with their team's cheerleaders. Their not-so-subtle dig lit a fire in me. We beat Savonlinnan that night and I was named player of the game in front of 9,000 fans. My reward was . . . a paper bag full of raw fish. Strangely, SaPKo's player of the game was given a trophy. My linemates were pissed. They took the fish and threw it against the rink wall. Then they bought a bunch of beer and we spent the four-hour ride back to Kirkkonummi drinking on the bus, my teammates cheering me up.

Always being a seeker can put you in some really uncomfortable positions. But it's the best way to grow—and there will be bright moments, too. Patches of sunlight that break through the over-whelming feelings of *What did I just get myself into?*—like my first goal for Salamat, or when my teammates had my back against SaPKo. Those moments will keep you going through the rough patches. There was another bright spot in that long year: Matilda Nilsson, the five-year-old daughter of Camilla and Toni Nilsson, the couple who ran the rink in Kirkkonummi. Matilda, who always wore a bright blue Salamat toque atop her long, white-blond hair, was a little rink rat. Her parents could never get her off the ice.

Matti, our coach, didn't seem to mind. He ran practice from the bench, never once lacing up to skate with us. When he blew the whistle, we'd skate to the boards where he'd explain the next drill. That was also Matilda's cue. At the sound of Matti's whistle, she'd hop onto the ice and race for the net, practising her shot on the suddenly empty net. When Matti whistled to signal the start of the next drill, Matilda would hustle off the ice and sit beside him, watching us skate.

Matilda came to every home game—she was practically our mascot. When things went badly, I would hear a shy little knock on my dressing room door. I'd quickly compose myself and let her in. She'd sit beside me. She didn't speak much English and I didn't speak any Finnish. But that didn't matter. We spoke the language of hockey. She'd smile up at me, and I'd feel my pain melt away. She was this brilliant, dazzling light in a very dark winter.

I've stayed close to the Nilsson family in the years since I left Finland. They've visited Noah and me in Calgary, and I've been back to Finland to visit them. In 2020, shortly after Matilda turned 23, she was named to the Finnish national women's hockey team. The little girl who sat with me in some of my loneliest moments all those years ago is now living out her own hockey dreams. I couldn't be happier for her.

- We grow by taking chances and putting ourselves in uncomfortable situations.
- Work with people who are bigger, stronger, faster, smarter. If you're always chasing, you will inevitably get better.
- Embrace the struggle bus!

7.

HARNESS
THE DOUBT

Face fear, then forge through it

In February of 2020, I was partway through my final year of med school. COVID-19 was quietly spreading throughout North America and I happened to be on the front line, working in ERs across Toronto as a clinical clerk. Watching the pandemic unfold right before me was frightening, surreal, and, admittedly, fascinating.

In the early days, before the terror set in, clerks didn't know enough to get too worried. I was naive, since not only was this my first foray into medicine but also, like so many of us, my first pandemic.

When the first COVID patient came through my hospital's emergency room doors, my supervising doctor did not want to even go into the examination room. They didn't feel adequately protected against the virus. It was too early to understand what precautions were necessary and effective. We didn't know what we were dealing with.

As the virus quickly spread, the attitude shift among physicians went from *Well, this may not be all that bad* to full-blown concern. A kind of free-floating anxiety settled over the hospital as the wards flooded with patients and systems were overloaded. And then, in the span of two days in early March, everything changed.

Within 36 hours of that first COVID patient's arrival, both hockey and medicine slammed to a halt. I was heading to the rink one morning, with plans to work a shift in the ER that night, when I got the call: clerks were being pulled from their clinical rotations. When I got to the Leafs training facility, I learned that the team was halting practices and the NHL was on hold. It was a shocking, confusing time. Everything was happening so fast. We weren't even able to return to the rink until safety protocols were implemented. Every speaking gig I had dried up. Like so many people around the globe, my entire life shut down in a span of 12 hours.

It left me feeling helpless. How was I going to pay bills? Should I go home to Calgary or stay in Toronto, ready to return to my hospital work and my job with the Leafs? Like my fellow clerks, I was just trying to get through my last year of medicine, graduate, and enter residency. Would the previous three years have been for nothing if I wasn't able to finish my degree? Was I ever going to finish medical school and become a doctor? What would happen to hockey as we knew it? I certainly wasn't alone—people around the globe were feeling the same way. We were all struggling with uncertainty and the feelings that were welling up in us and preventing us from thinking clearly.

I was worried about my parents, both in their 70s. I missed Noah, who was at university in B.C. It shocked me how alone I felt, with my family far away, and I was so unsure of what my next move should be. Above all, I felt purposeless. I was chomping at the bit, wanting desperately to get back into the hospital to help people who were suffering.

That's what had drawn me to medicine in the first place: a desire to help people in need. To try to put them back together. My obsession with medicine started shortly after my relationship with hockey began.

When I was 10, my next-door neighbour Alyssa, a little girl a few years younger than me, was badly injured after being run over by a grocery delivery van. I remember going to the hospital to visit her with a bunch of kids from our neighbourhood. She was going to be okay, and it was a huge relief. Aside from how scary it was to see one of us so badly hurt, what stayed with me from that visit was watching how the doctors and nurses cared for her. They were slowly, gently fixing her, while we all sat around and watched. It was inspiring. I wanted to be just like them.

Some people were surprised by my move into medicine after I retired from hockey, but that was always my plan. As a kid, I dreamed of going to Harvard University to play hockey and study medicine. After I retired and announced my next pursuit, I kept hearing the same thing: "Medicine, now? Aren't you too old?" But I'd been preparing for this second career for decades.

I started my undergrad in my early 20s—and I didn't finish until 2013. While I was playing for the University of Calgary, beginning in 2010, I completed my bachelor of science degree and then a master's degree in medical sciences. I wanted to be ready for med school once I was retired from hockey.

In early 2020 I was living in Toronto so that I could spend my mornings at the arena with the Leafs and my afternoons and evenings in the ER—yet another of my meticulously laid plans, one that traffic and subway delays routinely threw off schedule. But that was nothing compared to the pandemic. When COVID hit, all of my carefully scheduled goals slammed to a halt.

No one knew how long the lockdown would last. So much was unknown, there was so much doubt and uncertainty, and it was all filling me with anxiety and dread. I didn't know what to do with myself, but I had to find a way to release my frustrations and fears. Freaking out about my life unravelling wasn't getting me anywhere. I needed to let myself really feel the fear and frustration, to worry the absolute crap out of everything so that I could try to move past it. Otherwise, I was going to get mired in it. You can get lost in there.

I set a timer and gave myself 20 minutes to worry over every little thing that was running through my mind. I agonized over the career setback I was facing. I brooded over the sudden loss of income and how it might impact me in the months and years ahead. I let myself run through all my fears for my family and feel all my loneliness and uselessness. During those 20 minutes, I listed all the worries eating me up and all the nightmare scenarios that might yet occur. I leaned into every fear I had, all the pain I was feeling.

I had started using short "freak-out sessions" to give air to my anxiety early in my career, when I was feeling overwhelmed by things I couldn't control. I would let myself stress out over every little thing that could possibly go wrong—but only for 20 minutes. Sometimes, it helped me recast my fears or see them in a different light. Other times, it showed me that these were just stories I was telling myself—that things really weren't as bad as I was making them out to be.

Once my 20-minute timer went off that day, I parked my fears. I poured myself a glass of red wine (a big one!) and let myself be grateful for what I still had. I find that when all else fails, finding things to be grateful for is a useful way to centre yourself. It's how I always follow up my worry sessions. I take out a piece of paper or make a mental note of all the things that are going well in my life, all the things I feel grateful for.

After that (first!) COVID freak-out, I forced myself to focus on the many good things I had going in my life. My family and I were healthy and relatively safe. I had savings that I could draw from if it came to that. I didn't let my mind go back to the worries I had let out. Instead, I brainstormed ways to fill up my newfound spare time that were productive and would make me feel like I was accomplishing something.

So, I ramped up my training, cranked out workouts in my basement gym, and spent hours on my bike, processing and thinking—my "moving meditation," as I like to call it. We started online training with Leafs prospects. I hosted Instagram Live chats to pass along hockey tips. We pivoted WickFest, my hockey festival that hosts 7,000 players each year, to a virtual event. I spent three hours every day studying medicine. Oh, and I wrote this book that you're reading!

I also gave myself some space to reassess my situation. I wanted to move away from the obvious and look up and around me. My life, as I knew it, would be altered for at least the next six months, possibly longer. I decided to stay in Toronto, where I could jump back into hockey and medicine quickly if I was needed. My family was safe and hunkering down, my son returned home from university. As much as I wanted to see them and be near them, I needed to be where I could be useful and make a difference. I just had to find other productive ways to use my time until I could go back to the hospital and the rink. I needed a new way of looking at my situation.

When things aren't going our way, our instinct is often to try harder. To dig deeper. In hockey, as in life, this can often be counterproductive. The urgency to make up for lost ground often means you're not seeing the open ice. You're passing the puck too quickly and it gets picked off.

It's often better to curl back into your own end, to take a breather—backing away from a problem before diving headlong into it. This gives you time to assess the situation and proceed deliberately, at your own pace. I did this in hockey all the time. When I was circling back with the puck, what I was really doing was giving myself the chance to read the ice and find an open path. Hockey is such a fast game. That's why pauses tend to make your opponent feel so uncomfortable. The best players have the ability to slow the game right down in order to fly past a player or create space to make a play.

When COVID struck, I intuitively backpedalled. I was circling my own end, looking for an opportunity where I might make a difference. Usually, my schedule is back-to-back-to-back. Suddenly, there were no deadlines, no tests, no obligations.

Admittedly, it was a little terrifying. But it also felt pretty great: I had a window of time to do something entirely new. When I found my opening, I pounced.

Early in the lockdown, doctors kept telling me how important it was to protect ourselves from the virus. One ICU doctor I know told me a story about how, during SARS, a patient of hers went into cardiac arrest and stopped breathing. A team of doctors and nurses ran into a trauma room without gearing up first—all except her. She took the time to put on her mask, goggles, and gown. And everyone who ran in ahead of her unprotected ended up getting SARS. She did not. In the end, one died from the virus. It really messed her up. You can never let your guard down.

My doctor friends were deeply concerned that there would be shortages of personal protective equipment (PPE) in hospitals and nursing homes. I texted that same doctor, the SARS veteran who is now the chief of a bustling intensive care unit in Toronto. I asked her how bad COVID was by comparison. Her response was chilling: this was going to be far, far worse. In her hospital, they were already running out of PPE and their ICU was full. The sudden, massive demand for PPE had led to widespread shortages. In a panic, some people started hoarding it, even stealing it from hospitals.

I am lucky to maintain a bit of a public profile from my playing days. So, in April, I launched an online plea for PPE. I offered to personally pick up the items (with proper distancing measured out with a hockey stick, of course). In return, I would give anyone who donated a signed jersey, a smile, and guaranteed good karma. My friend, the actor Ryan Reynolds, saw my tweet and jumped in to help.

Ryan and I have known one another for several years; we met at an awards ceremony and bonded over our shared hatred of them. They are so stiff and formal—I'd rather be picking rocks in a field. That day, we were both being inducted into Canada's Walk of Fame. I'd brought a special guest: a nine-year-old hockey player, Grace Bowen, and her family. I'd met Grace at SickKids hospital a few months earlier; Grace was sick with osteosarcoma at the time and died a few months later.

As the evening began, my family was huddled together with Grace's in the corner of the lobby, hiding like the small-town farmers we all were. Ryan came over and introduced himself. When I saw the way Grace's eyes lit up, I took Ryan aside and we conspired to surprise her.

When I brought her on stage, I asked Grace who she was most excited to meet that evening. "Ryan Reynolds," she said, without missing a beat. Ryan leaped out of his chair, jumped on stage, and gave Grace a kiss on the cheek. It was all I could do not to break down right there on stage. He made this little girl feel like the most special person in the room. Ryan and I have kept in touch and helped one another with various projects. We share a love for kids, and both Ryan and his wife, Blake Lively, do a huge amount of good in the world. He's funny as hell and a truly lovely human being.

When Ryan saw my PPE tweet, he amplified the request to his 35 million Instagram followers, boosting my call for masks, gloves, and chemo gowns. Anyone who stepped up to help, he said, would receive a personalized video or picture from Deadpool, one of his best loved characters.

Within 24 hours, we had legit replies from 300 people all over the world willing to help. (Deadpool swag is far more exciting than a signed jersey from me, I have to admit!) We also joined forces with Conquer COVID-19, a group of physicians, business leaders, entrepreneurs, and other volunteers working to ensure frontline workers had access to masks, gloves, and other essential supplies. Together with a group of 200 volunteers, mostly folks who had never met before, we helped raise $2.36 million over eight weeks, delivering more than three million items of PPE across Canada. This turned out to be a much-needed initiative. When Justin Trudeau was asked eight months into the pandemic his one regret about how he'd handled it, he said it was that Canada hadn't had enough PPE in the early days. I smiled hearing this, knowing that all the effort and hard work Conquer COVID-19 had put in really mattered, and probably saved a lot of lives.

As Conquer COVID-19 was taking shape, I was also in the midst of co-founding a business called Pandemic Solutions. The company helps manufacturing plants and small and large businesses figure out how to get back to work—and keep running safely— during a pandemic. We do everything from providing cohort software to tracking and tracing solutions and implementation plans to ensure that employees and the people they serve can stay safe. One of our first major clients was Bombardier, the multinational manufacturer of jet airplanes and rail equipment.

The volunteer work combined with getting a new business off the ground and virtual Leafs work kept me going until I was able to get back to the hospital in July. Returning was a relief. But my first month back was sobering. Unsurprisingly, life had changed, perhaps forever.

I noticed a major uptick in overdoses. A lot of family violence. A lot of mental health calls. People were coming in sicker than they should be; they were waiting too long to seek treatment, often afraid to go to a hospital. A few weeks after my return, I treated a young person who had spent three months in the intensive care unit battling the lingering effects of COVID. Being bedridden for so long had taken a huge toll on this young patient's body. I'm not sure they will ever recover to full function.

There were days when my brain felt like it might explode trying to absorb all the new information that I was learning about the virus. My hands became red and cracked from washing them as many as 75 times a day. The mask took some getting used to; I wore one at least eight hours a day. I worried about getting COVID—who wouldn't? But that is what I signed up for. I was really proud to go to the hospital every day and see how hard everyone was working to stay safe and care for the sick. My doubts from back in March hadn't disappeared, and new ones arose all the time. There were still days when I had to give myself a few minutes to worry. Those fears and doubts will never go away. They are part of life. But we can learn to harness them and move on.

A big part of being human is learning to fend off doubt. It's something I do on the daily. If I'm completely honest, I let that fear drive a lot of my life and decision making. It affected everything I did. The good thing is, once I recognized it, I knew I needed to let it go, and I found a way to do it.

In my playing days, I knew that every day I went to the rink I was going to be told something that needed to be improved upon. The coach would tell me to execute better. My trainers would tell me I needed to lift more or work on my flexibility. Nothing was ever good enough, and though that's part of working towards a goal, it can be so completely draining when the reminders feel constant. When you're told day in, day out that what you are doing is not good enough, it can spur a lot of doubt. When I was most obsessed with chasing perfection, it led to my being consumed by doubt and fear.

Denying those feelings won't make them disappear. I've found that it's better to recognize my fears—whatever it is that I happen to be going up against. So, I worry. I lean into my fears. And then I park them and move on.

- Give yourself a few moments to let your fears wash over you. Then let them go.
- Take a step back to gain a different perspective and find your opening—your opportunity—in the chaos.
- When all else fails, finding things to grateful for is a useful way to centre yourself.

8.

EMOTIONS AREN'T THE ENEMY

Emotions have power—use them

When I was a kid, I was high-strung, to put it mildly. My emotions lived right at the surface. When I lost or didn't get my way, I melted down. I'd get hot as a furnace, throwing loud, ugly tantrums. I always played physical, impassioned hockey and had a tough time controlling my emotions into my early 20s. It was to my detriment and I had to focus on learning how to manage my emotions, to not let them overpower me. These days I am very composed, and was for the latter part of my hockey career, but I can still tap into that wild, emotional side when I need to.

The thing is, emotions have power. They are not your adversary. You just need to find a way to put them to work for you instead of allowing them to work against you.

—

Team environments can be tricky, and emotions tend to spread from one player to another. When the team is up, positivity is infectious. But when you are in a rut, it can be difficult to snap out of it. Emotions can make a great flashpoint, if you use them intentionally.

I remember the first time I tried doing that. I was furious. We were at Rogers Arena in downtown Vancouver. We'd just finished playing Sweden ahead of the Salt Lake Olympics. It was a bad, bad night. We'd managed to beat the Swedes—by a single goal. We didn't deserve the win. At the time, Sweden wasn't strong enough to compete with us, and we should have blown them out of the water.

The vibe was dark. It was a shitty time. Our coaches were berating us after sloppy practices. They were refusing to set the Olympic roster, leaving everyone in the lurch, wondering if they were going to make the cut.

We'd been playing like garbage for weeks, losing seven in a row to the U.S., losing to a dozen midget boys' teams, losing, losing, losing. Our power play wasn't producing. The penalty kill was a disaster. We'd tried shuffling the lines. Nothing seemed to be working. We weren't gelling as a team and we were stuck in a deep rut.

That embarrassing game against the Swedes was my last straw. I'd had it. As I walked off the ice that night, all I could think was *Enough*.

It was dead quiet when I opened the door to the dressing room. No one was talking. No one dared turn on the stereo. The girls all sat in their stalls, heads down, silently undressing. The mood was heavy.

Nancy Drolet was the first to break the ice. "Come on, guys," she said. "It's not that bad."

I lost it. "Not that bad?" I shouted. "Not that bad? We almost lost to Sweden!" I just kept going. I was undressing while I was yelling, hurling my elbow pads and shin pads at the floor for emphasis. By the time I was done, I was standing in my sports bra and spandex in the middle of the dressing room, breathless, panting.

The entire team and coaching staff were blank-faced, staring at me.

Okay, so this was not my proudest moment. But I maintain that it was exactly what we needed in that moment. We needed a jolt of emotion to knock us the hell out of that rut.

We were being complacent. I was exhausted by the BS excuses we'd been making for ourselves. Nothing wasn't getting through to us. The message needed to come in a more primal form.

When my rant was over, I didn't feel embarrassed. I didn't worry that I'd said the wrong thing. I felt relieved. I'd said my piece. I'd told the team what was in my heart. I could live with myself. I felt like a big burden had been lifted off my shoulders. I'd been feeling that way for a long time.

It's okay to lose it once in a while. It's like a pressure valve: you need to let off some steam every now and again. But it has to be carefully controlled and come with intention. And it's never okay to berate someone. I was pissed off about our performance as a team, and I included myself in that. I wasn't letting myself off the hook. I was playing like shit, too, and I told the team that. I didn't single anyone out. I never did. It is never okay to tear a strip off someone in front of the team.

Hockey is a game that has to be played with passion. You can't play the game numb. Energy drives change. Emotion drives performance. And it would be a shame to exclude emotions from your game—we all have them. It's a part of being human. But there's a fine line between being driven by emotions and being in control of them.

As a kid, I didn't regulate my emotions very well. I was undisciplined, hot-blooded, impulsive. I had big highs and profound lows. When things were hard for me, I didn't wallow; I got angry. I got so wound up one time that my mom sat me in a chair in the kitchen mid-tantrum, pulled out the spray hose from the sink, and hosed me down to cool me off. You remember the story from the first chapter: I didn't stay sad when we lost in Nagano, I was boiling with rage.

Shannon Miller, my first coach on the national team, used to tell me that I was like a wild horse that needed to be tamed. I had so much emotion bubbling away inside me, threatening to explode. I thought that being a little wild on the ice made me a good player. I was right, to an extent. I would never have become the player I was had I been emotionally flat. I needed to play with passion to be at my best. But strong emotion is a double-edged sword. It can be harnessed as a force for good when you need to light a fire in your team. But a lack of control can be a detriment. When I was full of passion and playing physical, I could get too riled up and take retaliatory penalties. I chirped the ref. I couldn't get a handle on myself and it hurt us.

When Wally Kozak, my X-Treme coach, saw that happening, he intervened. He could see that I was letting my emotions get the better of me. We sat down together at the rink watching a practice, talking it over. He told me that he was worried that I was too focused on who I was as a hockey player. It wasn't good for me or the team. Having only one focus, centring myself solely on hockey and not having any other outlets, was okay when things were going my way on the ice. When they weren't, my reaction was disproportional. It made every failure on the ice momentous. He was right: all I cared about was winning and improving my game. It wasn't healthy, nor was it sustainable. Wally was gently pushing me to take a wider approach to my life—to find passions outside the rink, to recognize that I was more than just a hockey player. He knew it would help me dial back my fiery reactions on the ice.

"Watch guys like Mark Messier," he said. "Watch his demeanour in a game. Looking at Messier on the ice, you'd never know whether his team was up by five goals or down by two." Under pressure, Mark was always steady as a church. I realized how valuable that was for his game and his team. When I was yo-yoing between joy and rage, my opponents knew when and how to get under my skin. I was becoming my own worst enemy by giving the opposition a soft spot to target.

It wasn't easy to hear this. It was embarrassing. Wally was calling out my behaviour. The worst thing was, I knew that he was right. Wally was a teacher and a father figure to me. I knew he said what he did because he cared about me. He wanted to help me develop as a player and as a person. He was someone I turned to when I needed help. I took every word he said to me that day to heart. I didn't want to make any more mistakes, and I trusted his advice. I was young still—19 or 20—and I instinctively felt what he said was right. He knew what I had to do before I understood it myself. I wanted to do right by him and my team.

This was one of the toughest things I had to master in my career, and it took me a long time to figure out. I needed balance; I needed to create more emotional outlets. I needed to find a way to not get so caught up in outcomes, win or lose.

Part of gaining control over my emotions was the simple process of growing up. I developed the maturity to understand that the way I'd been behaving was detrimental to the team. When you're in the penalty box, your teammates are upset. You're harming the performance of your team. I needed to calm down.

With experience, I saw that when I managed to contain my emotions, it gave me the upper hand. Wally helped me see that when the other team was out there trying to rattle me, trying to get under my skin, they were playing distracted. They weren't focusing on the puck.

I didn't have to let them distract me. I had the power to stop myself from reacting. I realized that the more cheap shots I received, the more I held it together in the face of their garbage, the more irked and angry they became. I was able to turn it back on them.

I also wanted to be a leader on my team. Before I was made captain, I knew I needed to start acting like one. I didn't think my teammates would want someone who kept flying off the handle in that position. I wouldn't.

So, I found strategies to manage how I react to my emotions. I focused on what I could control: my preparation, my attitude, my discipline. I planned ahead. I tried to stay consistent. This helped me manage my nerves. I didn't focus on the reffing or trash talking. Those things were beyond my control; fixating on them was a distracting waste of energy.

I tried to keep things in perspective. If I had a shit game, I reminded myself that's all it was—a single game. I needed to keep training hard, keep outworking my opponents, keep studying our systems. When I had a bad shift or got scored on, I would get back to the bench, take a huge drink from my water bottle, spit it all over the ice, and let it go. It was a silly little ritual, but it helped me to refocus and move on instead of obsessing over a mistake.

It's not easy to figure out how to make your emotions work for you. And no one can teach you how to do it—we're all different. Over time, I managed to do a complete 180. No matter what was happening on the ice, no matter how far behind we fell, I kept it together. I still played with the same degree of passion—that wasn't ever going to change—but I no longer let my anger get the better of me. I'd found a kill switch.

In my latter playing days, I had a bit of a Jekyll and Hyde thing going on. On the ice I'm intense. I will run you over if I need to, no fucks given. I'm there to play for my teammates and my country and will do what it takes to win. Off the ice, I'm pretty laid-back, reserved, quiet, shy even. I am naturally an introvert, though my public life doesn't allow me to be. As much as possible, I try to conserve my energy and my brainpower so that when I have to be out there in the world, I can give it everything that I have.

Giving yourself a moment to breathe before reacting can be a huge help. In hockey and in life, I have a strict 24-hour rule for phone calls, text messages, or emails that anger or irritate me. If you've got a kid in minor hockey, you know this rule well. It's become a mantra in the youth game. You've probably had to use it a few times while standing at the boards. It's a good rule. The world is moving at hyper speed, and a lot of people react, especially in writing, without really thinking through what they're saying. If I'm upset, I wait a full 24 hours before replying. In taking a breather, I'm letting the dust settle to gain some perspective. I always end up cooling off and coming back with a sober, rational reply. No matter the issue, it never seems as irritating or enraging a day later.

I implemented the rule several years ago after making a pretty stupid mistake. It was everyone's worst email nightmare. Gah, it still makes me cringe! I had been approached by another country's women's national hockey program; they wanted to hire me to assist in their development. Before long, however, it became clear that they weren't seriously interested in hiring me; they wanted intel and a free development proposal. I fired off an angry email ranting about the situation to my agent and my communications advisor—or so I thought. It turns out I had also cc'd the head of that country's development program.

Lesson learned. The hard way.

Emotions don't affect only us—they leach out and change the mood around us, whether in the dressing room or the office. Which is another reason why learning how to manage them is crucial, especially if you're in leadership. That said, you can use your emotions to shake things up and change the vibe for the better. Humour can be a magic fix. When we had a laugh together as a team, things never felt as bad or stressful. It was a great equalizer—the rookie who'd spent most of the game riding the pine could laugh along with the first line centre who could barely catch her breath. It helped us connect as a group.

When you're playing hockey for Team Canada, trying to win a gold for the country, your days can feel so stressful. You're fighting for ice time. You're fighting to make the cut. You're competing against your teammates. Your coaches are always watching you, judging you. No one can endure that kind of heaviness day in, day out. That's why I always valued team clowns. Jokesters were integral to every team I played on. They know exactly when to crack a joke to cut the tension and get everyone smiling again.

At one training camp, the coaches were super slow in making the final cuts. The atmosphere was tense and heavy. We decided we needed to relieve the pressure. We'd been divided into two groups, practising one after the other. Our group had been on the ice first, and as we headed off we sent Brianne Jenner, the youngest rookie, into the dressing room first. Brianne was super quiet at the time— shy, polite, sweet. She *hated* to swear. We told her to go in the dressing room, chuck her helmet, drop a bunch of F-bombs, and slam her stick against the wall and the rest of us would follow. Brianne let her inner actor loose. Caroline Ouellette went next, tossing her gloves on the floor, and then we all staggered in, repeating the drill.

The second group looked at us like we all had three heads. What had happened out there? Were they in for the worst bag skate of their lives? We had them going for a few minutes. Then one of them figured out we were messing with them, and we all had a good laugh.

Positive energy can have the biggest impact; when everyone feels appreciated, they perform better. Ahead of Salt Lake, our team environment got pretty tense after the coaches decided to put five forwards on the power play. No defence got the nod. Usually, on the power play, you have three forwards and two D or four forwards and one D. It's rare not to have any defence at all on the PP. The defence took the slight to heart and were super down about it. They felt the forwards were being given all the opportunities to shine. It created divisions and rifts within the team. You could feel that the tension was getting to a breaking point.

As a leadership group—the Olympic veterans among us—we could see how it was affecting the D and our team as a whole. So we decided to host a "D Appreciation Day." We had the slogan written on T-shirts. We made the defensive unit dinner and gave them a manicure and pedicure, possibly the single most useless beauty treatment for a hockey player. It was a fun, relaxing night and it helped bring us back together as a team.

It was like sticking a pin in a balloon: it deflated a lot of the tension and anger and heaviness that had built up. It helped dial down the intensity overall and changed our team energy as we headed into the Salt Lake Olympics. A few weeks later, when one of the D was moved onto the power play, we celebrated her promotion as a team.

Making emotions work for me is never about tamping them down or repressing them. They have too much power for that. Emotions just need to be put to work for you, not against you.

- Emotions are great fuel, if you harness them rather than allow them to harness you.
- Focus on what you can control: your attitude, preparation, discipline.
- When people feel appreciated, they perform better.

9.

THE THINGS WORTH FIGHTING FOR

Do what's right, not what's popular

One day in early December 2020, as the second wave of COVID-19 was ravaging Alberta, I arrived for a shift clerking in a Calgary ER. Ten minutes in, a code blue call came: paramedics were on their way with a critical patient, an overdose victim. He was in diabetic ketoacidosis, a potentially life-threatening complication of diabetes. We didn't know his COVID status. It took an hour to stabilize him.

I was just leaving his bedside when I overheard one of the nurses say, "There's a guy in the ambulance bay sat-ing at 48 percent," meaning his oxygen levels were less than half of where they should be, low enough to cause a coma or seizure. Somehow, the patient was alert and responsive. I just shook my head. A normal blood-oxygen saturation is at least 96 percent—48 percent is insane.

Unlike a lot of other respiratory illnesses, this coronavirus can starve the body of oxygen without causing people with the illness much shortness of breath at first. Without the patient feeling the changes to their body happening, it starts shutting down. Such infected patients—like the man in the ambulance bay who'd come in with an extraordinarily low oxygen level yet somehow was still blithely chatting with doctors—are known as "happy hypoxics." Sometimes their blood is so oxygen depleted that their lips and fingers will be tinged blue, yet they are still smiling and breathing normally. The scariest part is how rapidly many will then deteriorate. They'll be looking fine, then you turn around to read their chart and they're suddenly unresponsive and in respiratory distress. At that point, they need serious and immediate interventions to save their lives.

That's what happened to our COVID patient that day. Within 20 minutes of his arrival, doctors had him on 60 litres of oxygen per minute, the upper levels of what a patient can safely be given. When I walked past the trauma bay 30 minutes later, two physicians were trying to intubate him. He needed to be sent to the intensive care ward, but the ICU in our hospital—the largest in the province—was full. There wasn't a single bed to spare. This patient was in no shape to be moved to another facility, so doctors had to make a call. The overdose victim we'd treated first was critical but stable, so they started calling around to city hospitals, trying to find him a bed in another facility—no small task with the city's adult hospitals running at 107 percent capacity. They eventually found a place for our first patient, and the

COVID patient was given his bed in the ICU—just one example of the kind of frightening high-stakes juggling the pandemic demanded of physicians.

Before my shift ended three hours later, two more code blues, or critical patients, came in. A third patient arrived with a blood clot in their leg and a fourth had a heart attack in the ER. Finally, a 102-year-old was wheeled in. He was dying and was designated DNR/DNI—"do not resuscitate" and "do not intubate," meaning we couldn't pursue any aggressive interventions like CPR or breathing tubes to keep him alive. All we could do was manage his symptoms. For the next 45 minutes, I tried to keep him comfortable and held his hand as he lay dying beside me.

I was wearing a plastic gown, mask, goggles, and surgical hat. Every part of me was covered in plastic. *I must look like an alien*, I thought. I felt a wave of sadness wash over me. Before they take their last breath, a lot of patients feel scared. They're searching for a bit of humanity—a shared smile, the warmth of an ungloved hand. Because of COVID-19, I couldn't offer him even that. He wasn't at risk, of course, but his children, who later joined him, were. I felt defeated when I left him.

As I stood in the hallway outside his room, I felt like I was standing in the eye of a hurricane. Paramedics and a doctor whizzed past pushing a gurney. You could feel the anxiety in the air, like an electric pulse. It had been this way for weeks. Like the sound of coughing in the intensive care units at the height of the pandemic, the hum of anxiety never really went away. The nurses and doctors around me looked gaunt, pale, and burnt-out. All autumn, they had been working short-staffed and under extreme pressure. Instead of taking breaks, some were stealing a few minutes between patients to call the families of the patients they were caring for.

Being in the ER at the height of the pandemic could be exhausting. It could be unsettling, scary. But after not being able to be in a hospital for the first months of the pandemic, it felt good to help, to be of use. Because clerks risked spreading the virus and worsening PPE shortages, we had been barred from hospitals. I understood, of course.

What I could not understand at the beginning of the pandemic, still couldn't understand months later during the second wave, and will never understand was the obstinacy of the International Olympic Committee in the early days of the pandemic. In March, as the entire world ground to a halt, the IOC was still forging ahead with planning for the Tokyo Summer Games. Even after the World Health Organization designated COVID-19 a global pandemic, the IOC refused to postpone the Games. Every day, I woke up expecting to read its announcement. But it never came. Instead, I kept seeing assurances from committee members about how they were moving forward with planning for the 2020 Summer Games, how the Olympics could not be stopped.

As businesses and facilities started shutting down, my athlete friends were coming to me privately, telling me they worried about training for pre-Games qualifiers. Gyms and pools were closing. They would have to improvise new methods on the quick, risking infection by sharing weights and equipment, putting their families and the wider community at risk. If the Tokyo Olympics were going ahead, they had to keep training. They didn't feel they had a choice. It was their job; it was what they lived for. If Tokyo was a go for 2020, then they had to be as well. Meanwhile, my doctor friends were telling me how much worse the virus was than the public realized. They were scared and telling me they didn't know how to treat it yet.

It was a strange and intense collision of my two worlds: sports and medicine. And it carried on for days this way, as the IOC kept claiming the Olympics would go ahead as planned. My experiences on the medical side had already made it clear that the Games could not be safely held amid a global pandemic. My anger with the organization kept growing.

At that point, clerks like myself were still working in hospitals; we hadn't been sent home yet. COVID treatment plans were changing by the day. At first, it was thought best to intubate early. Then it was thought best to hold off intubation for as long as possible. There was some evidence that steroids could help. And there was evidence that laying people on their stomachs, or "proning" them, was effective. We found ourselves in a constantly evolving med school. The stakes were sky high.

In mid-March 2020, a fit, healthy young patient arrived in hospital. He was a non-drinker and non-smoker in his early 40s presenting flu-like symptoms and a shortness of breath. Initially, he seemed fine: he was upbeat, his vitals were good, and he was breathing on his own. But within a few hours, everything changed. He had by then been diagnosed with COVID-19.

He became confused. His breath quickened. His oxygen levels were sagging into the 60s. Then all of a sudden, he tanked. The team had to secure his airway, intubate him, and rush him to the ICU. The speed and ferocity of the virus left me shaken. He was the last person you would think would be taken out by COVID-19 to that extent. He had no pre-existing comorbidities, like asthma or a lung condition. Until then, I'd had this idea in my head that it was high risk only to older or immune-compromised folks. I was dead wrong. I couldn't believe how sick our fit young patient had become, or how fast it happened. It was a huge wake-up call. I felt absolutely sick, and the knowledge that Tokyo 2020 was forging ahead filled me with dread and anger.

That day, I took an informal poll of my closest doctor friends. "Could an Olympic Games be safely staged in July 2020?" I asked. Not one thought it could. "Are you insane?" one replied simply. This hardened my resolve. I felt compelled to take a stand.

The next morning, I woke early. I was sipping my first coffee of the day, worrying about the young patient—he was still intubated and struggling to survive—when I saw the latest tweet from the IOC, still insisting that the Opening Ceremonies would go ahead as scheduled in July. I couldn't believe what I was reading. Furious doesn't begin to describe it. It was so tone-deaf. I felt that the IOC's decision to forge ahead had nothing to do with the health and safety of the athletes but rather with everything else: money, posturing, politics, TV licensing deals, corporate wishes. Witnessing how quickly and drastically the virus had taken down the young man placed this headline in such a different light for me. It no longer felt merely irresponsible; it felt lethally dangerous.

That was my breaking point with the IOC. I couldn't just sit back with the knowledge and the experience I'd just had in the hospital; I had to say something. I have a decent-sized platform, and I was a member of the IOC Athletes' Commission, a peer-elected board that advises the Olympics' governing body. I was in a good position to voice my disagreement with the IOC's plans and call them out for what I believed they were doing wrong. I'd been elected to the commission to be a voice for athletes. Knowing they were feeling pressured to find ways to continue training in the midst of a global pandemic, I felt it was my responsibility to say something.

Voicing public disagreement with an organization as large and powerful as the IOC is no small matter. I knew my opinion would spark anger. But I couldn't stay quiet and live with myself. You have to do what you know is right, even if the consequences will suck. Early on in my life, when I got angry, I fought, I yelled, I raised hell. But I came to see that I couldn't willy-nilly fight every battle. I don't have the time or the energy or the capacity. None of us does. These days, I choose my battles carefully, when I know I can make a difference. When I'm trying to sort out whether or not to take on a fight, I ask myself, "Is this my battle to fight?" And "What difference would winning it make in the long run?" The most important question I ask myself is "If I *don't* take on this fight, can I live with myself?" That question is key; my conscience always plays a major role in deciding whether I fight or stand down. If I take something on, I take the time to gather my facts and make damn sure I have a constructive solution to offer—or a plan for developing one. I'm not in the habit of shooting off my opinion without an end goal in mind.

It's not a wise manoeuvre to go it completely alone when the stakes are this high. I had learned that as a team leader. Once, when my team was in conflict with a coach, I tried to deal with it on my own in order to protect the team, and spoke to the coach one on one. In the end, I got burned. I was labelled a "troublemaker" by management and had no one to back me up. The experience taught me that it's easier and more effective to take something on with people standing beside you.

Before I called out the IOC, I reached out to Olympic champions Mark Tewksbury and Beckie Scott, whose opinions I trust and respect. Both Mark and Beckie have extensive experience with the IOC's inner workings and are respected public figures in Canada. I told Beckie that I couldn't live with myself if I let this go another day. She and Mark agreed that I should speak out. They helped me craft a plan. We considered having a private conversation with the IOC to voice our concerns, but I knew from previous experience that it might not be effective. I was just one athlete and didn't have enough clout to sway them. By 2020, I had been with the organization for four years; I knew how they operated. Ahead of Rio, I had been involved in less public discussions with IOC officials over whether to ban a country from the Games for previous violations, and those discussions had gone nowhere. I felt they were just window dressing—done to make it look like the organization was considering it. I got the feeling that the decision to let the country compete had already been made. When it comes to the IOC, sometimes the only way to really force change is to have the public and media hold them accountable.

Just before noon, on March 17, I dropped this on Twitter:

> I've given this a lot of thought. I was voted to represent and protect athletes. As an IOCAC member, 6x Olympian and medical doctor in training on the frontlines of the ER, these are my thoughts on the @Olympics.

Everyone looks forward to an Olympics—fans, athletes, the media, the TV audience, the sponsors, and marketers. It's the biggest sporting event in the world. It would be a wonderful thing to look forward to. BUT this crisis is bigger than even the Olympics. Athletes can't train. Attendees can't plan travel. Sponsors and marketers can't market with any degree of sensitivity.

I think the IOC insisting this will move ahead, with such conviction, is insensitive and irresponsible given the state of humanity.

In the hours and days that followed, the message travelled around the world. I started doing interviews—Canadian media, CNN, BBC. I also heard from IOC officials. They were furious. They told me I needed to seek their approval before addressing the public.

Like a lot of organizations, the IOC likes to control the message. I get that. But I didn't feel that a democratically elected institution like the IOC should be censoring its members, especially at a time like this. And that's what the officials were doing by telling me I needed approval before making public statements. So, I told them I was in the role to give athletes a voice; I wasn't there to be told what to say. That didn't go over great.

To make a long story short, I said we could agree to disagree, but I strongly felt they were going to end up on the wrong side of history on this. I was working on the front line of this medical emergency, I reminded them. And I know the mentality of an athlete. If I had been preparing to go to Tokyo, I would have been doing everything humanly possible to keep training. I'd probably be taking undue risks. Any athlete would do the same.

Those tweets of mine took on a life of their own. Before long, prominent organizations including USA Swimming and USA Track & Field issued calls for a postponement, as did the Olympic committees of Brazil, Norway, and several other countries. Five days later, Canada became the first nation to declare that it would not send its athletes into harm's way if the Olympics were held that summer. "This is not solely about athlete health—it is about public health," said Team Canada in a statement. Australian officials followed shortly after.

Two days later, Tokyo 2020 officially became Tokyo 2021.

I feel like this took a huge burden off the Olympians. It allowed them the time to safely prepare. And why even have an Olympic Games when so much of the world is in crisis and can't celebrate? Everything was uncertain. The Olympics were no exception.

The postponement announcement was bittersweet. I sympathized with my fellow Olympians, whose dreams were delayed. But I also felt a sense of relief—that the IOC had made a safe, humane decision. Sport is profoundly important to me. But lives were at stake. There is nothing more important than that.

Looking back, I have no doubt that I did the right thing. That experience reminded me that there are things in life worth fighting for. I could sleep at night knowing I had spoken my piece about something fundamentally wrong; my conscience was clear. It also made me realize that one person can make a difference, even in the face of an organization with the heft and sway of the IOC.

The reality is, doing the right thing can come at a great personal cost. It can be lonely, isolating, painful. Is my IOC career over at the end of my term? No doubt. It is unlikely there will be any more commission spots or cushy IOC gigs for me. I know that. But I couldn't care less if I never go to another five-star hotel care of the IOC. And if my position in international sport is tarnished because I didn't toe the party line, so be it. All I cared about was doing the right thing.

Sometimes in life, there are two clearly laid-out paths ahead of us. I came across "The Road Not Taken" by Robert Frost in my mid-teens, and it's stuck with me to this day. It ends,

> *Two roads diverged in a wood, and I—*
> *I took the one less traveled by*
> *And that has made all the difference*

For me, voicing my opinion against the IOC and putting myself in an unpopular position was another road less travelled by, another example of how my life has turned out the way it has. It was not the popular choice. But I trusted my gut and did what I believed was right, consequences be damned.

- Standing up for the things you believe in can be lonely. Be true to yourself and unafraid to go against the grain.
- Take time to gather facts and have a constructive solution, not just an argument.

10.

FLYING COMPOST

Focus on what you can control; let go of the rest

The 2002 Olympic women's hockey final in Salt Lake City is best known for two things: lopsided refereeing and the lucky loonie secretly buried at centre ice. But when I think of Salt Lake, something else entirely comes to mind: Emerald Lake.

In the run-up to the Salt Lake Winter Games, we were practising eight hours a day, six days a week. We had started six months earlier with a gruelling six-week boot camp in Valcartier, Quebec, which was designed to whip us into shape. Our training regimen that year was intense, even for us. We had been through centralization only once before, but we had had countless small camps and competitions in the years before Salt Lake. Mitch Marner, currently an alternate captain with the Leafs, once told me that he'd started training with a few players from the national women's team. He couldn't believe what they had to do to fitness test. If an NHL star thinks our training and regimens are hard, it really tells you something. We spent three days fitness testing;

NHLers spend three hours at it. We knew what we were up against in 2002, though, and what it would take to succeed.

If there was ever a time that Team USA had a hand over us in our rivalry, it was in the lead-up to Salt Lake. Not only did they beat us in eight straight exhibition games, but they outscored us 31 to 13. They never played better. Their win in Nagano four years earlier had opened doors and cheque books at USA Hockey, which meant considerable funding for the drive for gold on home turf. They centralized for four years leading up to 2002. We had just six months together.

Those losses were eating away at us. Whenever we play the Americans, we're out for blood. Hate might be too strong a word for it, though on game days, it sure didn't feel that way. You get shot, you get hit, you get sticked, banged, and cut. Once I asked Bob Clarke what it was like playing against Russia in the '72 Summit Series. "Hayley," he said, "it wasn't hockey. It was war." That's exactly what it felt like playing against Team USA. This went deeper than hockey.

Our coaches worried that Salt Lake City's elevation—1,330 metres above sea level—might hinder our performance. Altitude tends to slow you down. The higher you go, the less oxygen your body delivers to your muscles, which leaves you feeling drained or sluggish. To build up our aerobic base, the coaches had us doing repeated sprints—on foot, bikes, and in skates. We were regularly starving our bodies of oxygen to prepare them to function with lower levels.

By the end of centralization, I think the organization recognized just how hard they were pushing us. Going into those Games was incredibly tense, and distractions were everywhere.

The press was openly questioning if our head coach, Danièle Sauvageau, was the right choice to lead us behind the bench. Executives at Hockey Canada were supportive but nervous. Just a month before Opening Ceremonies, following our eighth loss to the U.S., Sauvageau cut a veteran player in favour of a young star from the U-22 squad, Cherie Piper. The last-minute change unsettled us. All of this made for a stressful, turbulent run-up to the Games. We needed a break and to have some fun as a team. Shortly before flying to Utah, management sent us on a three-day retreat to a resort on Emerald Lake, just west of the Alberta border.

The milky-blue glacial lake is the jewel of B.C.'s Yoho National Park. The rustic, upscale lodge smelled of pine trees and woodsmoke, an ideal place to kick back for a few days. The only training that we logged was a game of shinny on a frozen lake. We were there to fill the tank.

Our bodies needed rest, but we couldn't neglect mental preparation. External pressures and inexperience had knocked us off our game in '98. We'd been undone by circumstances outside our control. On this retreat, we created a game plan for that, just as we would if we were facing a team that used a zone trap. We brainstormed a "distraction list": all the crazy things that could occur at the Olympics to distract us from our mission. We had almost 200 things listed on the whiteboard by the end: everything from the death of a family member to a terrorist attack to awful reffing in the final. Circumstances we would have no control over, things that could mess with our focus.

We decided that if any of those awful scenarios came true, we would say "Emerald Lake." Not the most original code word, but we were tired. Emerald Lake suited us just fine. It was a reminder that sometimes things happen that are beyond our control. You've got to roll with them regardless. We had no idea how valuable this simple exercise would wind up being.

The core of our 2002 squad were Nagano veterans. Cassie Campbell was named captain, with Vicky Sunohara and me serving as alternates, and beyond official roles, we had a core group of players who were the true leaders on that team. We had learned from Nagano not to limit our world to hockey alone. To stay loose and relaxed, we needed to schedule some downtime to have a bit of fun and think of something other than hockey.

Once the tournament started, we rolled through the round robin, outscoring the competition 25–0, with wins over Kazakhstan, Russia, and Sweden. We struggled against the Finns in the semi-final before turning things around in the third with a come-from-behind 7–3 win. That win set up another North American final.

When we met as a team on the morning of the gold medal final, the mood was upbeat. There was a lot of chatter, a lot of laughs. The puck drop was scheduled for 5 p.m. at the E Center in West Valley City. The arena is an intimate venue, roughly half the size of a typical NHL rink. I remember stepping onto the ice for warm-up that afternoon; it was like stepping onto the battlefield.

When I get onto the ice, the first thing I always do is look for my family. I saw my brother and sister—they were hard to miss. My brother was shirtless, and my sister was wearing a bikini top. Their chests were painted red and white. *Dear god*, I remember thinking, chuckling at the pair of them. I was thrilled to see them there and a bit taken aback by how proud of me they clearly were.

For days I'd been racked with nerves. But suddenly a feeling of calm came over me. Directly across from our bench were all these American flags. I smiled, took a deep breath, and said to myself, *Fuck it. Just play the game. You're ready.*

It's easy to go into a game when you are the underdog. It's so much easier to be the hunter than the hunted. When the puck dropped, it was as if all that pressure we'd been feeling in Nagano had been transferred to Team USA. When you're the defending Olympic champion and you've won 35 exhibition games leading up to the Games, there's nowhere to go but down. We felt that the game was theirs to lose. I could see the fear and pressure in their eyes at every faceoff. For the first time all year, they looked tentative, nervous. We just had to be patient and capitalize on the mistakes they were sure to make.

We rattled them by opening up the scoring just 1:45 into the game. Cherie Piper demonstrated exactly why Danièle wanted her in Salt Lake, grabbing the puck off the faceoff from the right circle, ripping around the net for a wrap-around. The puck deflected off goaltender Sara DeCosta's stick, but Caroline Ouellette, a lumbering power forward, buried it for the first goal. Our bench erupted. That early goal set the tone for the rest of the night. For the first time all tournament, Team USA, which had steamrolled the competition on the way to the final, was playing catch-up. We were on fire, playing better than we had in more than a year.

We had the momentum. But then things started to shift. We got called for a penalty. *Shit, we need a big kill*, I thought. The refs called another penalty and my heart dropped. *OMG, their power play is too good*, I thought. *We need to stay out of the box.* By the third penalty called against us, I was feeling like we couldn't sustain the pressure. By the fourth, we were reeling. The American referee, Stacey Livingston, kept hitting us with penalty after penalty.

We were losing the upper hand. You could feel our emotions rising on the bench. Everything we tried to do ended up putting us in the box. We were frustrated, furious, overheated, disappointed. It was starting to look like we were going to go home with the wrong colour medal once again.

Out of nowhere, Dana Antal, a soft-spoken rookie, spoke up on the bench right in the heat of the battle. "Guys," she said calmly, because that is her style. "Emerald Lake. Emmmmeraaaald Lake." Our bench burst out laughing. Of all the potential nightmare scenarios we'd listed that day in Emerald Lake, the final one on our list was coming true: awful reffing in the final.

With that, Dana turned a super stressful time into a moment of levity. She brought us back to that sweet, serene place in time. It was a reminder that, no matter how angry we got, the ref was the one holding the whistle, not us. We needed to simmer down and focus on what we could control. Dana's poise and levity in the moment made all the difference.

As the penalties kept coming, we went from a feeling of "Fuck you, ref" to "Okay, this is the way it's gonna be." By the sixth penalty, we were gaining a lot of confidence in our ability to kill them. We were almost laughing on the bench—the situation was so ridiculous.

In all, we had 13 penalties, playing almost half the game in the box.

Remembering Emerald Lake helped us regain our composure and get back into the right frame of mind. We couldn't change the situation. All we could do was play our game. Our confidence grew with every penalty we killed. The Americans, meanwhile, were panicking because they weren't scoring on the power play. I couldn't help but smile.

Because our penalty kill was one of the things we *could* control in that game. Going into the final, our PK had sucked. The Americans kept walking out from behind our net and sliding the puck across the crease to Cammi Granato for a back-door goal. It made me crazy. I kept thinking, *Why can't we stop this?* So, the night before the gold medal game, all the players on the PK got together with one of the coaches. We held a secret meeting in a basement room of the athletes' village. It was like a final study session. We used it to check in with one another and build trust and sort out how to shut down the back-door play. In that final, our penalty killers were overworked but never better.

Whenever I saw the Americans lining up their set play, I screamed "Back door! Back door!" to Becky Kellar and Cheryl Pounder, who were on the ice with me. We kept stoning them. I remember feeling so in sync with them. The Americans' power play couldn't make a cross-crease pass. It seemed to freak them out; they had been relying on that play. After shutting it down three penalties in a row, we knew we had shifted momentum back. The Americans deflated as their PP collapsed. They were getting tight and scared just as we were starting to feel loose and free.

We headed into the dressing room for the final intermission on a high. Just before the clock ran out on the second we'd taken a 3–1 lead on a breakaway goal by Jayna Hefford. It was a set play that began when Vicky Sunohara won the faceoff.

That was Heff's signal. She went flying down the wing, slipping behind the American defence. Becky Kellar sent the puck flying 100 feet. Hefford caught up with the puck and headed for the net. Hefford caught DeCosta leaning right, poking it past her with just one second remaining on the clock. It was an incredible goal and moment in the game.

The air came right out of Team USA's tires. We could almost hear the hiss inside the rink. The Canadian fans got a lot louder, and the American fans went suddenly quiet. We knew we were on the cusp of something great.

The third went by in a flash—we kept them at bay for the first 16 minutes. With just 3:33 remaining in the game, Karyn Bye managed to score, making the score 3–2. We didn't flinch. Bye may have given her teammates hope, but she couldn't give them more time. It's funny. It seemed that when nobody believed in us, that's when we finally started believing in each other. We were on fire that night.

As the final second ticked off the clock, we poured over the boards, chucking our sticks and gloves into the air and rushing for Kim St-Pierre, who was always cool as ice in those big moments, and in that one, she didn't let us down. She'd finished the game with 25 saves in a brilliant effort. Nagano was still agonizingly fresh in all our minds. The eight successive losses to the U.S. had humiliated us. But we fought back. We peaked at exactly the right time. It was Canada's first Olympic gold medal in hockey in 50 years. The healthy contingent of Canadian fans in the stands went berserk.

I was the first player off the ice that night. When I opened the door to our dressing room, Wayne Gretzky and Kevin Lowe, team managers for the men's squad, were standing there with big grins and open arms. It was an incredible moment for me. As a little kid, I had idolized the Oilers—and both of them. Here they were in our dressing room, telling us how great we'd played. What an unforgettable moment. The entire men's team had come out to support us that night. They later told us we had inspired them for their own showdown against Team USA three days later, for the gold. In that moment in our dressing room, I realized just how far the women's game had come.

We did it by playing our game. We had learned how to let circumstances beyond our control slide off us and focus on what we could: being the best national team in the world.

You can only control so much. When I played at the University of Calgary, the players I came up against were not Olympic-calibre athletes. Some would try to take liberties on me, taking out my knees or getting a stick caught up in my legs. They couldn't keep up with me and were using other means to try to slow me down. It was frustrating as heck: players ended up being reckless on the ice, and it was dangerous. If your opponents can't keep up with you, their goal can be to rattle you, to knock you off your game.

After a particularly aggravating game, my friend Syl commented, "God, there's a lot of flying compost on the ice today." I could not stop laughing. That's exactly what it was! "Flying compost" became our term for a player or team who couldn't keep up with you so they tried to beat you by being cheap. Playing against flying compost is a bit like being a decent dancer paired up with someone with octopus legs. It's awkward. You're out of step. It's not a lot of fun. But it's just one more thing you can't control. If you allow the flying compost to distract you, you won't be performing at your best.

Flying compost is a decent metaphor for life. I realized I have to let the extraneous noise and crap deflect off me. In our day-to-day life, we have to deal with people who are subpar, who we don't like or don't want to work with. As our team learned in the Salt Lake final, there's a lot of crap that can fly at us that we can't control. All you can do is ignore it. After a while, flying compost gets annoyed or tired or they hurt themselves. All you can do is keep your head screwed on and not end up in the compost bin with them.

• Accept that you can't control everything. Shut out the noise and refuse to let it knock you off your game.

THE POWER OF PLAY

You gotta love what you do

Late one night in the winter of 1985, my dad was having trouble sleeping. He kept hearing a strange knocking sound coming from outside. It was after midnight and minus 20. Finally, Dad went to check on it. When he got outside, he discovered what was making the noise: six-year-old me. I had slipped out of bed, laced up my skates, and was ripping around our backyard rink, working on my slapshot in the dark. Dad hollered at me, sending me flying back to bed. But he didn't deter me. From then on, I just made sure that when I snuck out at night, I was working on my stickhandling or skating—the silent parts of my game.

Anything that I became in hockey, I owe to that rink. Dad taught phys. ed., math, and science at Shaunavon's tiny high school, played in a rock band with some friends, and skated in an old-timers' hockey league. Dad was a lot of things, but one thing he was not was an elite hockey player. That didn't matter to me. I watched his games as if they were the NHL. We lived a few blocks from the arena, so Dad used to pull me there on a sled. There was no point in getting in the car.

"Dad, I'd like to play hockey too," I said to him from my sled one cold, dark night. "Sure, Hayley," he replied. He wasn't saying that to placate me. He got up early the next day to start building a rink for us. He was a stickler when it came to following through. If he told you he was going to do something, it was as good as done. Dad froze a path leading from the house to the rink. That meant I could lace up inside and then glide out the back door in my skates.

The backyard rink was my church and my first love. I lived out there. Every time my blades touched the ice, it was like I was being handed a blank canvas. I wasn't just skating. I was creating. I was dreaming. No one was criticizing me or yelling at me. I felt free and safe because that's where I belonged. I loved the feel of my blades cutting into the rock-hard ice. I loved the crispness of the air. I loved that I could see my breath. I didn't feel the cold, no matter the windchill factor.

Being on that ice wasn't work to me. Practising my stick-handling or skating wasn't work. It was fun. It was pure joy. The skills I gained came from a place of joy. Even as a kid, I loved to rise and grind. I loved the process of learning, improving, growing stronger. I knew that the day the pain and grind outweighed my love for the game would be the day I found something else to do.

—

The fun aspect of our lives can easily get lost. It happens all the time, not only in sports. People choose a career path based on something they enjoy. Then life kicks in, and with it the desire for achievement, progress. There are meetings, paperwork, deadlines. Aspects you don't love overshadow the fun parts. I found this with the national team sometimes. There were weeks when hockey felt like a no fun zone. The focus was on drills, endurance, systems. It was work, work, work, train, train, train. All. the. time. Our intention—to become the best we could—was something I believed in, but in pursuing our goal, we forgot the most fundamental part: why we wanted to be there in the first place. We forgot the joy. When our focus was purely on training, drills, and systems, I could sometimes feel my inspiration start to fade. It's hard to stay motivated if all you have to look forward to is another hour of a penalty kill strategy. When you work the game and grind for too long, you start to slow down. You get tired. You become less creative, less effective. I saw this lead to injuries and burnout with the national program.

Whenever I catch a few moments of a minor-league hockey game, I get hit with a rush of sweet memories. I can get lost there for a few minutes, remembering what it felt like to play so free. There were times when I needed to draw on those happy recollections—when I was feeling burned out or frustrated with the game and the politics that can suck the joy from it. I needed to remind myself why I had chosen this life. I had to find that joy again.

In 2013, when I was struggling through injury and living through a lot of upheaval at Team Canada, I dialled up Lesley

Redden, a former national team goaltender. There is no one in this world who loves to play hockey as much as Lester, who plays six days a week, year-round. Her joy and love for the game is as pure as any I have ever seen. I got her to meet me at a frozen pond in northwest Calgary. For a few days, that was the only hockey I played—shinny on that pond. I spent hours and hours there each day, breathing in the cold, crisp air, skating until my lungs burned and my hoodie was soaked in sweat. I needed to remind myself why I had committed so much of my life and self to this game. It wasn't for the championships or the medals or the awards. It wasn't to see how far I could take my game or how much I could accomplish. From the moment I took my first tentative strides on the ice, I fell in love with the game. I played because I loved it. I needed to find my way back there.

Joy changes us physically. Our brains and bodies need the hormones that flow only when we are having fun, creating, exploring, discovering new things. Fun can be as instrumental to a team's success as breakout systems. When we realized that, as a team, we started being diligent about having fun, hosting penalty shot competitions with goofy prizes or competitions to see whose music got played in the dressing room. For years, Cherie Piper, a Scarborough, Ontario, native with eclectic musical tastes and a knack for putting the puck in the net, held the job of team DJ. She made sure that our dressing room was a jamming zone, a fun zone. Even if we were going to be focusing on pure systems that day, we could bring good energy to the ice.

Ahead of the 2020 minor hockey season, as the pandemic cancelled some seasons outright, a lot of hockey parents in Canada worried about the impact of a "lost season" on their kids' games. I thought those fears were misplaced. Record numbers of backyard rinks went up across Canada that winter, and instead of regimented practices, kids devoted hours and hours to unstructured play on outdoor ice every day. Nothing could be better for their games.

Backyard rinks are no-pressure zones. There are no coaches, just kids playing the game however they feel is right. No one is there to judge, instruct, or criticize. The colder and the darker out, the more magical it always felt to me. It was a refuge, a place where I could escape into my imagination and be whatever I wanted to be. A place I could grow and fail and learn and take my game wherever felt right.

This joy and endless play makes kids better hockey players without it feeling like work. Instead of drills to teach them to make crisper passes, those changes and skills come to them naturally. My puck control came from playing endless games of shinny. I learned to react more quickly in the small spaces, and it injected creativity and artistry into my game. That little rink taught me that hockey is a game of angles and speed. I developed a razor-like precision to my shot—because missing the net meant wasting precious minutes digging the puck out of the snow. My accuracy didn't improve because a coach would skate me if I missed the net; it rose because I was shooting for the joy of it and concentrating on hitting the net so that I wouldn't have to go searching for the pucks after I ran out.

I firmly believe that shinny is Canada's secret weapon, the reason the country produces so many of the world's best hockey players. Pond hockey lets kids develop naturally, playing the game with joy and verve. They aren't gaining skills through repetitive and regimented drills. Their passing, creativity, and space recognition is improving through play.

My visit to Rio de Janeiro in 2016 for the Summer Olympics as a member of the International Olympic Committee's Athletes' Commission cemented this theory about how important play is. While I was there, I visited a *favela* where I saw a group of kids playing a game called futsal.

The game *looked* like soccer, but the ball was about half the size of a regular soccer ball. On a graffiti-covered concrete court the size of a basketball court, the kids were playing with blinding speed, making quick, controlled passes and beautiful, deft touches. Their skills were probably on par with national team athletes in Canada. I was entranced. I stayed for hours, skipping a couple of official engagements to watch the kids play.

Some were in bare feet. Some had running shoes on. It was 35 degrees in the shade. I was sweating just watching them. But the kids didn't seem to feel the heat. It was the same way we never seemed to feel the cold when we were playing pond hockey. This tiny concrete court, I realized, was their backyard rink. Futsal was their shinny.

It is also that country's secret weapon. Every great Brazilian footballer grew up playing futsal, which developed in the country in the 1930s. Some players didn't graduate to the beautiful game until they were in high school. I believe futsal helps explain why Brazil remains the greatest soccer nation on the planet in the same way that pond hockey helps explain Canada's dominance in hockey.

One reason for this is repetition: futsal players touch the ball far more often than a soccer player does in a game. Just as on small backyard rinks, the smaller court demands precision play. Kids learn to work their way out of tight corners with quick combinations and ball control. When futsal players graduate to soccer, they feel like they have miles and miles of free space. That's how kids who grew up on tiny backyard rinks feel when they step onto a full-sized rink. These skills aren't gained through drills or elite camps or playing the game year-round. They are gained through joy, play, and fun.

As a parent, I saw how powerful play can be for a child's growth when I moved to Sweden for the 2008–09 season to play men's pro in the Swedish third division. Being away from my family had been the hardest part about playing in Finland a few years earlier. We decided that this time Tomas, my partner at the time, and Noah, our son, would come with me. Sweden also put us closer to Tomas's family in the Czech Republic.

Eskilstuna, where we lived, is a former industrial city of 100,000, roughly 100 kilometres west of the capital, Stockholm. The team's sponsor, the carmaker Volvo, provided us with a home, two cars, and a salary. We enrolled Noah, who was going into grade four, at a local school. It rained a ton in Eskilstuna. The days were cold, wet, and dark. But the climate doesn't dampen the Swedes' enthusiasm for *friluftsliv*, which roughly translates to "living close to nature." Spending time outside is a big part of Scandinavian culture.

Outdoor free play, even in the coldest months of winter, is an essential part of Scandinavian childhoods. Every school day, Noah spent three hours outside, whether it was pouring, hailing, or dumping snow. His recesses were more frequent and longer than in Canada. He would get drenched and cold during these outdoor breaks, but each classroom had a row of heated lockers. When the kids came inside after playing in the rain, they hung their sopping rainsuits and boots in the warm lockers. When it was time to head back outside, they would pull on dry gear.

Noah's teacher told me that he noticed that his students were better able to sit still and learn after they spent time outside, moving around, and using their little imaginations. In the Swedish system, Noah spent roughly 80 percent of his day playing. To this day, my son's favourite place in the world is Sweden. I think it's because he had so much fun there. What Sweden taught me as a parent is that if you want your kids to learn to regulate their emotions and channel their attention, let them play. If you want them to be creative, innovative little humans, let them play. Whether you want to foster healthy development or help them reach the outer limits of their hockey game, let them play.

I came back from Eskilstuna a better hockey player. But by far the most valuable lesson I brought home was the crucial importance of play—and not just for kids. I think some of us go through periods where we take ourselves too seriously. I know I did as a young person. In my time in Sweden, I learned to ease up a little and take a more balanced approach to my life. Every mammal spends part of their day playing. It is in our nature. When hockey or life itself becomes a grind, the joy is excised from it. With that goes all the beauty, spontaneity, and creativity that elevates good players to great players, good teams to great teams, and good doctors to great doctors.

Life isn't just for working. When what used to be your greatest joy becomes tedious and a burden, you can't do your best work. We all get wrapped up in life and lose our passion sometimes. And that's when we need to go back and tap into why we loved something so intensely in the first place.

- If you want to foster healthy development in your children or help them reach the outer limits, let them play in unstructured, no-pressure zones.

- Every mammal spends part of their day playing—it's in our nature.

- When what you love the most starts to feel heavy, it's time to return to basics and find your bliss all over again.

THE
OFFENSIVE
ZONE

Time to let fly

WHEN YOU HIT THE OFFENSIVE ZONE in hockey, the goal is simple: you want to score. This is the moment of truth. If you've done the work, you can relax and let it happen. You don't have to try lifting the bar any higher: it has already been raised high enough. The building blocks are in place, and it's time to let fly and achieve great things.

While the neutral zone is about fine-tuning your approach, the offensive zone is where you trust in yourself and your preparation, in all your hard work. Ideally, in this zone, you should always be a threat.

There is a lot of freedom in the O zone. Finally, you can breathe. You can make decisions on your own. You can fake a pass, then drive the net. You can delay up high or low on the circle, patiently waiting for the opportunity to pounce—going slow to go fast, as I like to call it.

At this stage, you've got perspective that lets you appreciate all the good things your hard work has yielded. With that perspective comes confidence—to trust in yourself, to open up and be vulnerable as a leader, to accept the loneliness that leadership demands. Now is also the time to start thinking about the legacy you hope to leave behind and to plan for what comes next.

12.

PRESSURE
IS A PRIVILEGE

Pressure is your teammate

In the run-up to the 2010 Vancouver Olympics, the heat was on us. We were the hometown team, playing a game that in Canada can feel more like a national faith than a sport. It's ingrained in us from a young age; its rites are passed down from generation to generation. Its drafty, worn-out prairie arenas are cathedrals for the faithful. No other sport or pastime has managed to capture the psyche of Canadians quite like the game of hockey has.

This might help explain why hockey losses on the world stage can lead to bouts of national soul-searching. The failure of our team and the men's hockey team to bring home a single gold from Nagano in 1998 ended up being discussed in Canada's Parliament. A national summit aimed at restoring Canada's supremacy in the rink was held the following year. Clearly, we take our status as the world's dominant hockey power seriously. Whatever humility people around the world expect of Canadians goes out the door when it comes to hockey.

Anyone who gets the chance to skate for Canada will tell you that part of your job is making Canada proud. Falling short is more than a personal defeat. It means letting down 38 million souls from coast to coast to coast. That's how it can feel, anyway.

Almost every day in the lead-up to Vancouver, our communications team prepped us to face questions from media about the "burden of pressure" that came with playing for gold on home soil. And thank god they did. Because in scrums and interviews, that's all reporters wanted to talk about. It's not like we needed reminding. We could feel the weight of the nation bearing down on us like a five-tonne truck.

It is so much easier to be the underdog. The U.S. was the underdog in '98, we were the underdog in '02. In my mind, it is no coincidence that the team that won gold in each of those Games was the one feeling the least amount of pressure. We arrived in Vancouver in 2010 with a two-Olympic streak of gold, which made us the team to beat. There was no getting around it. No quick fix like "Emerald Lake" to relieve the pressure. We had to find a new way to not get overwhelmed.

Instead of trying to release the pressure, we decided to embrace it. We turned to Billie Jean King. The tennis great was 22 when she won her first singles championship at Wimbledon, the first of 39 Grand Slam titles. When reporters asked her how she coped with the stress and pressure, she often said: "Pressure is a privilege. It only comes to those who earn it."

King was bang on. It's an immense privilege just to be in a position to feel that kind of pressure. Not just anyone is given the opportunity to carry that load. The country was demanding great things from us because they believed we were up to the task. We needed to respect that. We couldn't let it intimidate us.

"Pressure is a privilege" became our mantra and our defining slogan. We focused team-building activities around that philosophy. Our team psychologist, Peter Jensen, ran training sessions around it. He would talk with us to bring out our fears, our hopes, and our insecurities, often by walking us through a series of worst-case scenarios. Peter forced us to re-examine the stories we tell ourselves. Was it really true that the gold medal final in Vancouver was the most pressure we would ever face in our lives? No, we realized, probably not. Was it really true that the country was going to feel like we had let them down if we lost gold? No, we realized, that wasn't true either. They wanted us to win, of course, but they wouldn't hate us if we lost.

When we talked about the weight of the nation bearing down on us, Peter had us flip that notion on its head. Instead of feeling the expectation weighing heavily on us, he had us think of it as pushing us from behind. Rather than fear pressure, Peter helped us recognize that a home crowd could be the proverbial seventh man on the ice, propelling us forward. If we fell behind, we could lean on the crowd and draw energy from them. They were there to lift us up, to carry us. They weren't there to weigh us down. This was our house. And this was our time.

When I played softball in the 2000 Summer Games, I was on the other side of the fence. There were no expectations on us. No one thought Canada stood a chance of winning gold in Sydney. Frankly, no one cared. That was difficult in its own way: to perform our best in a competition that no one cared about. People putting pressure on you shows that the outcome is important to them. It shows that they care. Even at the Olympic level, few athletes get the chance to play in front of a sellout crowd that desperately wants them to win. Especially in women's sports. It's an amazing thing to get to experience.

Before my second hockey World Championship in 1997, I had never played in front of a packed arena before. That year, the Worlds were held in Kitchener, Ontario. We were set to play the final in front of 8,000 fans. I remember feeling incredibly nervous before I got out onto the ice. And yet at the same time, I was so excited to play in front of Canadian fans.

I told myself, *These are your friends. These are not your enemies. They are on your side. They want you to do well.* Looking back, I see that I was already reimagining the things that scared me the most, repositioning stressors as strengths. By reframing pressure-cooker situations, what feels overwhelming and unmanageable can suddenly feel like an opportunity.

In the lead-up to Vancouver, we thought, *Holy shit. Everyone will be watching. Half the country thinks we're going to effing choke.* And we had to tell ourselves, *No way. They're with us. And you know what? They're going to make all the difference.*

That could have felt really scary and intense. But we had reframed it.

When I hit the ice for our first game in Vancouver, I looked up at all the flags, all the people in their red and white jerseys, all the people with their faces painted, all the girls in the stands.

And I thought to myself, *All these people are here for us. All these people are on our side. All these people want us to win.* And I recognized what an incredible privilege it was just to be there. This was something people dream about. I got to live it.

It's important to do things that scare the shit out of us, that cause us to feel the most pressure. These happen to be the things that will push you to your absolute best. They will also be the things that most excite you.

The truth is, the pressure in Vancouver was nothing new for me. It was heightened from playing on home ice, but I felt that level of pressure at every Olympics. For me, the four or five days before the gold medal game were always absolutely agonizing. I would lie in bed at night thinking, *Why did I choose this? Why am I torturing myself? I could be on my couch right now, napping, watching TV.* I would be stressing about getting the team to the semi-final. Then for the next two or three days after the semi, I'd be stressing about the looming final. The nights felt endless. I felt like the only one who stressed out to this extent.

Until Peter Jensen told me about one of his former clients, a world-class Canadian figure skater. When this skater was under intense pressure, he would think, *I don't want to be here. My back hurts. I hate this sport. I never liked figure skating to begin with.*

Turns out, it was very normal, the way I was feeling with pressure bearing down on me. Peter told me that a lot of athletes go through these phases, of being unsure why they started in the first place. It's okay to be not okay. It's okay to worry, to let pressure fill you. But you had to give it an exit; otherwise, it could lead to an explosion. I found ways to cope. I built in some time in my Olympic schedule to let myself ruminate about losing the gold—the "freak-out sessions" I described earlier. I would tell myself, *Okay, between 2:30 and 3 p.m., you're allowed to panic.* I leaned into it. I walked through each disaster scenario. I accepted that losing was a possibility. And then I stopped, let it go, and rested.

It turned out that the agonizing, the anxiety, and the panic were just another part of my Olympic routine. It was just a thing that happens. A process that I went through, however uncomfortable. Eventually, I came to realize that being successful in moments of intense pressure was, above all, a battle of the mind. It was the strongest competitor I would ever face—in sports, business, or any other facet of life. Some people tend to shy away from that sort of thing. I tend to pile it on. I have always put way more pressure on myself than anyone else has. My parents sure didn't. The only thing they ever asked of me was that I play piano until grade six. I wasn't allowed to quit until then. (What a nightmare!) They seemed to understand that I was already high-strung. That I was already driving myself hard. They didn't need to add to it.

When I start to feel pressure building in me—my heart rate quickens, my anxiety rises, I start to feel self-conscious, self-critical—I know I need to get outta my head. I need to resituate myself. I shift my attention to the ground or my skates. I focus on them completely. I breathe in slowly, deliberately. Sometimes I scrunch up my toes, then relax them while I'm breathing in. I use these deep breaths to get out of my head and back in the present, into my body. I remind myself it's normal to feel pressure and okay to not always feel okay. Embracing the pressure makes it a friend, not an enemy. It turns this big scary thing from a mob of people waiting for you to fail to a group of supporters cheering you on.

These days, I do something similar as I'm practising medicine. The first time I was doing a paracentesis—draining fluid from a patient's abdomen by puncturing it with a needle—I was super nervous. I was sticking a catheter into someone's belly, trying not to perforate their bowel, using an ultrasound to help me guide the catheter into place. The stakes were high. If I punctured the patient's large intestine, I could have caused serious, potentially life-threatening damage.

A paracentesis is not an overly complicated procedure. But the first time you do anything, it's nerve-racking. I had an internal medicine physician standing beside me, watching me. Having someone keeping an eye on every move you make and judging you is unsettling. This guy, however, said something that put me instantly at ease: "I'm right here. If anything goes sideways, I'll be right here to talk you through it."

I'd been feeling a boatload of pressure to perform the procedure properly. But as soon as he said that, I recognized that he wasn't there to add to the pressure I was already feeling. He was on my side. He genuinely wanted me to succeed—if only because it would be a giant headache for him if I screwed it up!

Whether it's fans, supervising physicians, colleagues, or managers, it can feel intimidating to know that all eyes are on us in a high-stakes scenario. It doesn't make you weird, weak, or not good enough to feel that pressure. It's something we all go through.

Remember, pressure doesn't have to be a burden—it can be your greatest teammate. The people around us want us to succeed. The country wanted us to win gold. The physician wanted me to complete a paracentesis on my first attempt. Pressure isn't the enemy—it is earned.

- Embracing and re-framing pressure changes it from an enemy to a friend.
- People around you aren't waiting for you to fail, they are hoping for you to succeed.

13.

EASY SPEED

Trust in your preparation

When we are pressed for time or stressed out, we tend to revert to the habits we know best. Sheer pressure or an intense pace prevents us from thinking clearly; our bodies have time only to react. That's why it is so important to have good habits. That's why athletes train so much. When you're in a final, whether it's at the Olympics or the NHL, and shit hits the fan and the pressure is unrelenting, you do the things you always do. Those automatic reactions you built as you earned a PhD in your sport or passion take over. All the training I did might have looked over the top to an outsider, but I was raising the bar each and every day so that when I got to the Olympics, I'd grown used to competing at the very highest level, consistently. My reactions were hardwired into me.

You can't just step into the Games and hope for the best.

This was never more apparent to me than it was in Utah. We stepped onto the ice for the final against the U.S. in Salt Lake City to chants of "U-S-A, U-S-A." The crowd was decked out in red, white, and blue. One thing the Americans do better than any other country in the world is patriotism. Salt Lake City was absolutely steeped in flag-waving and nationalism. With just five months having passed since the 9/11 terrorist attacks, the Americans used them as a galvanizing force in those Games, and rightfully so. One of the players on the USA women's hockey team had lost her father, a bank analyst, in the World Trade Center. All of this made the moment even more poignant and emotional for Team USA.

Unbeknownst to us, Salt Lake officials had battled with the IOC for permission to bring a special banner to the Opening Ceremonies: the tattered American flag that had been recovered from the wreckage of the World Trade Center. An honour guard made up of firefighters and police officers who'd been on the ground in Manhattan on September 11th carried the fragile banner into Rice-Eccles Stadium. I remember standing in the holding area waiting to walk into the Opening Ceremonies and seeing President George W. Bush rush past.

The moment the flag was carried in, the only sounds in the massive stadium were the whirring of camera shutters and the thrum of helicopters overhead. The silence hung thick in the air. Then the Mormon Tabernacle Choir, clad in white, began softly singing the national anthem. It was a wrenching moment.

The wave of patriotism and resilience that had lifted the U.S. in the aftermath of the attacks helped power American athletes to a record 34 medals—roughly the same number the U.S. had won in the three previous Winter Games combined. It was a spectacular Games for America.

Given all that, you'd think that going up *against* the U.S. for the gold medal would have been intimidating and intensely stressful.

Particularly considering how we had lost spectacularly to them in Nagano. The truth is, once that puck dropped, all the tension faded from my body.

In the lead-up to the final, I'd been a wreck. For 10 days, I was anxious, worried, and racked with self-doubt. At the Olympics, there's too much time to think, so many hours spent waiting. The Americans had owned us that year. Their power play was white hot. They were a machine. That might have been the best American team I've ever seen in an Olympic Games. Every time I did an interview, I was asked to defend why I still thought we could win. It was exhausting.

I felt a huge responsibility to bring my very best game to the final. In hockey, your top players have to perform in the big games. There's no way to win without them. All of that was churning inside me, all of those doubts: *Can I do this? What if we lose again? Is the world going to think we're chokers? Failures?*

And then heading into that gold medal game, I stepped on the ice and looked up into the stands. American flags and face paint were everywhere. "Here we go."

As my skates bit into the ice, a sense of calm came over me. The stress and uncertainty and pressure lifted. I felt confident and in control. It was like being a kid again—like I had boundless energy and passion. I felt like I was flying out there.

You might think that it's in these moments that the pressure is the highest. When the game is the least fun. The truth is, by the time we get to the gold medal game and actually step out onto the ice, that's when I finally start to relax. The gruelling work of the past four years is behind me. All the preparation, sweat, dead lifts, sprints, and pain are done. I knew I hadn't skimped on any of it. I had done everything humanly possible to ready myself for the 60 minutes that lay ahead. I'd trained hard, almost too hard. I'd eaten well every single day. I was diligent about getting enough sleep every night, even while caring for a toddler. Now, it was time to leave everything I had on the ice.

I came to call the Zen-like sense of calm I felt in those moments "easy speed." With easy speed, everything is flowing. The game no longer feels like work. Your muscles don't get tired. You're floating out there, weightless. It's like you could skate forever. Your mind is clear. You are not burdened by the weight of expectations, pressures, hopes, desires. You have boundless energy and can tap into it in ways that you never thought possible. Easy speed comes with surrendering your expectations and fears about the outcome and fully embracing the moment. You have the confidence that comes with knowing you have done everything you can to get to this place. Nothing feels forced. If you have ever experienced it, there is no denying its magic.

I came to know that poised, serene feeling I first felt in Salt Lake well. It returned to me every time I stepped onto the ice for the gold medal match in the three Olympics that followed: Turin, Vancouver, and Sochi. In those games, I would look into the crowd and find a Canadian flag or jersey. I would focus on it for a few moments. In that time, I would appreciate how goddamned blessed I was to be there. I would tell myself, *Feel this, enjoy this, remember this. No matter what happens, this is what you live for.*

Knowing I was ready helped me move into that mission mentality. There were no nerves. I was in control. The waiting game was over. The training was done. The hay was in the barn, as we say in Saskatchewan. It was time to trust in my preparation and let fly. A big part of easy speed is mental—getting yourself to that relaxed state. But the key is doing the work early, so that when the moment of truth arrives, you can relax and let fly.

Getting to easy speed came from many, many years of honing my craft. I was only able to tap into it when I deeply and truly believed in myself. And I could only ever feel it when I had found an inner peace. To mount a great performance, I had to be at peace with myself, know myself, and believe in myself. That's when I was able to find that glow, that light, that next gear.

I saw easy speed in Usain Bolt when he ran the 100-metre sprint in Beijing in 2008. I was down at track level with Clara Hughes, the champion cyclist and speed skater, for his race. Over the years I've had the opportunity to do some cycling and training with Clara, who also trained at the Olympic Oval in Calgary. We have similar philosophies about sport and life. She is probably one of the most driven, focused, positive people I know.

During the race, it looked like Bolt was floating on the track. Clara and I just turned to one another, mouths agape. We both knew the feeling. Twenty metres before the finish line, Bolt let loose, throwing his arms wide, thumping his chest, a look of pure joy spread across his face.

When I got back to my hotel that night, I watched the replay over and over. The faces and jaws of the guys running beside Bolt were clenched, etched in pain. They were trying so hard. Their muscles were tight. They looked scared.

I've been there, too. That's the opposite of easy speed. When you're stuck there, it's like skating through mud. Nothing flows.

The game feels impossibly hard. You can't relax. There is no glide. It's as if you're fighting against gravity.

A lot of people get overwhelmed in big moments, when it is go time. They panic. They feel that they need to perform perfectly, better than they have during any practice, that they need to put on the performance of a lifetime. What this tells me is they don't feel ready—for whatever reason, whether it's that their training wasn't enough or that they have a mental block preventing them from fully relaxing into the moment.

If your preparation before game time has been good, there is no reason to be overwhelmed by pressure when the puck drops. If you've trained your body and your mind, and raised the bar every day, there is nothing to worry about when the game is on the line. If you have practised and prepared until all the habits you need are established and your skills have moved from conscious to automatic, you've already done the hard part. The gold medal final, that's when the fun starts. You can fall back on your training and just do what you practised. Nothing more, nothing less. You don't need to pull off something extraordinary in the moment—just do what you've prepared yourself to do.

- When we are stressed, we revert to the habits we know best—good or bad.
- Easy speed comes with surrendering your expectations and fears about the outcome and fully embracing the moment.
- Being fully prepared lessens the pressure when the puck finally drops.

14.

LEAD FROM THE HEART

The heart carries the feet—lead with it

It took me a long time to figure this out, but being open and vulnerable with your teammates can endear you and connect you to the people you're trying to lead. That's an especially important lesson to learn if you're stiff and rigid and controlled all the time like I was as a leader.

Like all of us, so much of my behaviour stemmed from the environments I grew up in. When I was still playing hockey with boys, I felt like I had to be twice as strong as the guys on my team. I learned from a young age that if I showed weakness, I wasn't going to be wanted. No doubt that shaped the person I became. Hiding any vulnerability was also part of farming culture; there was this mentality that you do what you need to do to get things done, no matter the cost. Your back may be aching, you may feel anxious and depressed, but you're also behind on seeding and so you push on. You do the work, and you don't "complain." This is changing more and more. These days, there is a big push to talk about mental health in farming communities.

I've come to recognize that hiding your vulnerable side isn't actually healthy. Nor is it a sign of strength. It may *seem* like you're tough if you swallow your feelings. The reality is that anyone can do that. What takes real courage is admitting to the people around you that you're suffering. Being vulnerable in front of a team is not something I have always been comfortable doing.

I chose very early in my career to leave hockey at the rink and lead my own personal life. I never engaged in the drama or the gossiping that was always going on in the dressing room. I hived myself off from it. I liked going to the rink, playing hockey, being a good teammate, and then getting the hell away. Back in the early years, I had a different life from everyone else: I had a little guy waiting for me at home, so I couldn't go out to the bars or hang out at night. I was the only player on the team with a child.

After Noah's birth, I started feeling disconnected from my teammates. I was hanging onto my energy and sanity by a thread as I tried to manage motherhood, sleepless, colicky nights, and the reality of parenting a sick child at 21. I needed all the energy I could muster to get to the rink, perform, and then go home to recover enough to do it all over again. I stopped hanging out after games—I just couldn't afford the toll on my body and mind. It was hard for my teammates to understand why I wasn't spending my time the way I used to, partly because no one else was a mom. But I also didn't open up to them. At the time, it didn't even occur to me that I could. I was under a ton of pressure: to be a good mom, to be the best player, to lead the team. I didn't show my teammates the pressure I was feeling or confide in them about my fears. In my eyes, they needed me to perform and to be a leader who brought it every day.

My distance and disconnect sometimes came across as coldness, remoteness, or disinterest in the group, but I think that those who really knew me understood my behaviour. I hope so, anyway. Back then, I wasn't great at verbalizing what was happening with me, but I got better at it as the years went on.

It was late in my hockey career that I learned the importance of vulnerability in leadership. The 2013 World Championships in Ottawa gave me a hard-earned lesson, one that left some scars.

I'd tweaked a bulging disc in my lower back in a practice, causing it to flare up at the worst possible moment—just as the Worlds were about to begin. By the time the tournament started, the pain was so bad that I could barely walk. Nighttime was even worse. I would alternate between lying in pain on the couch and pacing my hotel room, trying to loosen up my back. The Ottawa Senators' doctor had to inject a high-dose steroid medication and anaesthetic into my spinal canal just so I could play. It was so bad that I was scared I might never play again.

I didn't want to disrupt the team and our preparation. Nobody likes a distraction. So, I decided not to tell my teammates what I was going through. I hid the magnitude of my injury from them; I tried to quietly manage the pain. I also didn't want the story getting out: the last thing we needed was the Americans learning that I was playing hurt. I assumed that our head coach would let my teammates know some downplayed version of the truth, but that wasn't the case. I didn't learn until after the tournament that he chose not to share any information with them. This made things so much worse.

In hindsight, our whole approach was a mistake, and it backfired. I should have been open about how bad the injury was. For the rest of the tournament I was hunkered down in my room, stretching my back, icing it, heating it, massaging it, resting it, doing whatever I could to get it well enough to play. I was trying to conserve my energy and focus on getting my body to a functional state. In doing so, I isolated myself. I didn't hang out with my teammates—no playing cards or watching TV in their hotel rooms, or even attending strategy sessions before the games.

The reality is, pain changes you. You don't think clearly when you're in pain. You're not sleeping right. You don't make good decisions. You're irritable, emotional. In this case, the pain I was feeling blinded me to the ways my actions could be misinterpreted by my teammates.

My unexplained absence created needless anger, tension, and divisions within the team at the worst possible time. They didn't know why I wasn't around, and they felt like I was being selfish and acting entitled, as if I had my own set of rules and could show up when I wanted. At the same time, I had no idea that they were in the dark about my injury. The reality was, I couldn't even walk. But they didn't know that, and I didn't know that they hadn't been told why I wasn't attending team meetings.

Then we lost the World Championship final to the U.S. in front of a sell-out crowd at home in Ottawa. It was in the lead-up to an Olympic year, giving Team USA a psychological leg up over us going into Sochi. It was the start of a pretty ugly stretch for Team Canada. Of the next 60 exhibition games we played to prepare for the Olympics, we won around 20. It wasn't just the team having issues; management was also being switched up. Our head coach suddenly exited the national program and was replaced by someone we didn't know, throwing the team into turmoil. When Worlds were over, the finger-pointing started. Some of those fingers were pointed at me.

Four months later, we centralized in Calgary. There was still a lot of lingering resentment and hurt over what had gone down in Ottawa. I decided that I needed to address it and shoulder the blame for it. While it wasn't my fault that we lost the World Championships, there had been a communication breakdown, and I felt that I needed to admit to the error and accept responsibility for it. I wanted a clean slate going into the Olympic season and to make absolutely sure that my teammates understood I would never try to run my own show.

None of us go through life without making mistakes. It's a painful but fundamental part of being human. Mistakes can also help you move forward: you make a mistake, you learn from it, you move on. I recognized that before we could move on as a team, I needed to take responsibility. I hadn't been the leader they needed at Worlds. I decided to write a letter to the team, expressing how I felt I should have handled things in Ottawa and what I thought I could do to become a better leader.

In it, I told them that I recognized that I could be guarded, that I didn't share enough of myself or how I felt. I told them that I was sorry and that I wanted to become a different kind of leader. I wanted to open the doors of communication in hopes that it would make the team more comfortable in sharing how they were feeling.

I chose to read the letter aloud. And I choked up. A lot of my teammates were like, "Whoa, we've never seen that side of you before." What I had to say was emotional. I'm often perceived as someone who is strong, who has it together. I was letting them see a different side of me. After 20 years on the national team, this was the first time I showed vulnerability and shared emotional parts of myself.

So much of what you hear from folks in leadership roles these days is finely polished, and hockey culture is still pretty reserved and conservative. That's a big part of why it can be so refreshing to hear emotion from a captain or a coach. Not just because it's rare, but because it's real. Being vulnerable and real and taking inventory of your limitations shows people a different, softer side of you. It aligns you with them. It's empowering.

I wasn't trying to hide anything that day I read my letter to the team. I was being me. A lot of the time, we think that hiding our emotions makes us look strong and in control. What the incident with Team Canada showed me was that in hiding my pain and the extent of my injury, I weakened my capacity to lead and put up barriers between my teammates and myself.

Being phony isn't being a leader. Most people have finely tuned BS meters and can see through the fakery. My teammates needed to see honesty and vulnerability from me. They needed to see that I wasn't always keeping it together. They needed me to acknowledge my flaws and be real with them.

In the end, that letter changed my relationship with the team. A lot of my teammates came up and thanked me for saying what I'd said. Some of them gave me a big hug and said they had no idea what I'd been going through. "That couldn't have been easy, Wick," Meaghan Mikkelson said. "I have a lot of respect for you saying that. It's what the team needed."

It was really hard for me to do. But it helped release a lot of pent-up pressure. It felt liberating and freeing. Being unafraid to be real and honest shows strength. That's leadership.

Another mistake that I made as a leader was trying to fix things or do things on my own. Eventually, I realized that it's better to empower other people on the team to shoulder part of the load themselves. It's really important to give people outside the leadership group the space and opportunity to step up and shine. As a leader, there are times when you need to be out front, dragging people by the neck along with you. At other times, you need to sit back and empower others to step up and lead, while you act as the engine of support. I call it leading from behind.

One particular failure came on the last day of boot camp in Dawson Creek in northern B.C. in the spring of 2009. At boot camp, or "Hell Camp," as some of the girls refer to it, we saw each other at our worst—bruised, burnt-out, frustrated, unhappy. You learn to rely on one another. You build trust in each other. That's where I fell down.

At the end of each camp, there is always a race. Individually, each of us was ferociously competitive. So, put us all together in a race and you can imagine how important coming in first becomes. Some girls even took swimming lessons ahead of camp to improve their stroke. Beyond innate competitiveness, there was another dynamic at play: camp was always held before final roster cuts. The coaches were closely watching these races. The stakes were really high.

On that day in Dawson Creek, we were divided into teams for a four-leg cycling and running race in the mountains. Each player on the team was responsible for one leg of the race. I was chosen to take the final bike ride. Partway through it, my bike broke down. One of my teammates, who had completed an earlier portion of the race for our team, came up behind me on her bike and offered to finish the race. I was the stronger cyclist, and my goal for the day was to win the adventure race. So, I did what I thought was the best thing for the team. "I'll take your bike," I said, grabbing it from her. All I cared about was who crossed the finish line first. We won the race, but I found out that my teammate was crushed that I didn't believe she was capable of doing the job.

That wasn't my intention. But it was a crucial in-the-moment mistake for me. I didn't think of the ramifications of my actions or really listen to her. Earlier in her career, she had been an impact player; at that point, her minutes were diminishing. She was very sensitive about it. But I wasn't thinking of the wider dynamic. It turned into something that we had to work through as a team.

It would have done a lot more for our team as a whole if I had taken up her offer and let her ride the final leg for me, showing her that I had confidence in her abilities. Sometimes, bringing the entire team forward is more important than doing everything yourself.

—

I learned a similar lesson as a mom. I wanted to let Noah make mistakes and figure things out on his own. That's how my parents raised me. They didn't pave a path for me or hover over me; they let me make my own decisions, for better or for worse, sink or swim. As much as I wanted to protect and shelter Noah, I knew from experience that I needed to let him fail. (And oh my god, if there is a worse pain than watching your kid fall flat on their face, I don't know what it is.)

When Noah was a teenager, he told me that he wanted to join the cadets and then the military as a reservist. I was surprised. I didn't know if it was going to be the right fit for him. Noah is honest and honourable and has always had a lot of integrity, but he is also a free thinker. He's quiet. He likes to keep to himself. He doesn't suffer fools. Though I wasn't sure if it was going to work, I supported him. I let him choose his own path.

He spent years and years in the cadets and was hugely successful there. He told everyone he was going to pursue a career in the military. I cringed a bit inside each time—from motherly concern and because I worried that it might not be the right fit for him forever. Eventually, all on his own, he tried something else for a semester and recognized that it was the history of the military, the knowledge, the structure, the discipline that really drew him in. By trial and error, he realized that military and art history are his true passions. Had I tried to step in and tell him what to do, I know I would have made things so much worse. I was glad I let him figure out his own path.

Empathy is a tool I learned to rely on only later in my career— almost too late for hockey. It didn't come naturally to me.

My coaches and teammates always expected a lot from me. I had to grow up fast to meet their expectations. I joined the national team as a 15-year-old and was installed on the first line with Angela James and Stacy Wilson. I was still in my teens when I was made an assistant captain. By 23, I had three Olympics under my belt.

I'd also come up in hockey at a time when coaches used fear, threats, and humiliation as motivational tools. Some were screamers. They kicked garbage cans across the dressing room or broke hockey sticks against the bench to make a point. They would demean players in front of the whole team. Some were drill sergeants who skated us until we puked to let us know how upset they were about a performance. They thought it would light a fire in their players, push them to perform.

Coaches got away with this behaviour because it was so normalized. Few players dared speak up in fear of retaliation. A vindictive coach could reduce your ice time or make your life a living hell. I'd seen it happen to my friends. I had it happen to me.

What I never saw was a coach looking inward, admitting fault in their behaviour or showing empathy for what players were going through. Or treating their players like human beings with lives outside the rink.

Hockey is changing, thankfully. The old-school, hard-ass coaching mentality I came up in is getting called out for what it is: toxic. People are recognizing the harm it causes. Like so many things, such toxic coaching has a ripple effect. It creates a culture of fear and silence, of never being able to speak out. In a sporting culture that expects complete obedience to coaches without question, a lot can get hidden. So when coaches' behaviour goes far beyond being tough, players are so entrenched in this culture and in fear that many stay silent. Abuse and racism are kept hidden or continue unchallenged by other people in a position to speak up. I'm thankful for players like Akim Aliu and Sheldon Kennedy for speaking out about the racist abuse and sexual abuse they suffered from coaches. They are paving the way for other players to come forward with their own testimonies of abuse and misconduct. There is no place for harassment or abuse in the game.

I try to be part of the change I want to see in the game. When I see a player within the Leafs organization struggling, instead of yelling at them, I ask them what's going on. Instead of labelling someone a troublemaker, I try to understand what is causing them to bring negative energy into the room or onto the ice. We have these conversations in private; I would never ask someone to confide in me in front of others.

Medicine, far more than hockey, has helped me build my humanity and understanding of other people's life experiences. A few times, I've cried with families receiving bad news. I think you do a disservice to yourself and your patients when you are unwilling to show emotion, if you are a blank face conveying horrible news. The doctor I was working with the first time I cried in front of a patient told me to be myself, whatever that looked like. She taught me it was okay to cry.

I'm still working on building my empathy muscle. When I first meet a patient whose body has been ravaged by disease or addiction, I still sometimes think, *How could this happen?* Then I catch myself. Because as soon as they start telling me their story, I understand what led them to this point. They faced abuse or grew up in poverty; they've been fighting serious health problems their entire lives. People have so many layers and are often facing so much more than what you can see at a glance. You can never assume you know the whole story.

By and large, my leadership approach didn't change much over the years. I'm not a rah-rah-type leader. I made sure I was training the hardest, working the hardest, that I was always on time and focused on becoming a better player and evolving my game. I wanted to set the example, particularly for younger players. I felt that by setting the standard for work and intensity, I didn't need to be loud.

From a buy-in standpoint, you can't expect your team to put in the work and training if you're not showing them the way. Even the CEO of a major corporation should be willing to get down in the trenches with her team. How can you lead if you can't relate? If I wasn't the fittest player on my team, how could I ever say a word about training and hard work? I had to back it up. But I also came to understand that not everyone operates in that same capacity. Or wants to. I couldn't expect my teammates to adhere to my personal standards.

I needed to listen to my teammates. If they were pushing back or having trouble keeping up, I had to stop and ask myself: *Am I being too demanding? Am I asking too much?* And I needed to dial it back when I was.

Checking your standards doesn't mean lowering them. It means approaching the people on your team from a place of empathy, and sometimes asking: Is this demand realistic for the person we're working with?

Before Sochi, a young player showed up to camp not having trained all summer. You can tell in 10 seconds flat how hard someone has prepared for the season. It's in the shape of their body, how red-faced and out of breath they get in the first drill. This player is an incredible talent but was notorious for having zero work ethic. She came to camp unprepared, showing disrespect for the program and her teammates. The coaches wanted me to talk to her.

Before I approached her, I asked myself: *Who is this person? Where does she come from? What has her life been like? What is it like now? Is she maxed out? Is there something else going on behind the scenes?*

When I took her aside, I wasn't a hard-ass and I didn't berate her. I told her I recognized something was going on in her life, asked her questions, and showed concern. I wasn't giving her a pass, but to be able to motivate and lead her and know what I could ask of her, I had to understand her. I learned she'd faced a lot of hardship. We talked about what she needed to do to get the training done and stick with the program because she is a great hockey player and we needed her on the team.

She turned it right around and is still with Team Canada today. Training will never be her first love, but she did manage to get her fitness to an acceptable level.

That said, I was never afraid to challenge people. It can lead to self-reflection, and from that comes improvement. After I was named captain of Team Canada in 2007, I wanted to help players be their best selves. I started to focus less on myself and more on the team as a whole, on getting the team to perform at a higher level and helping players be their best.

I often pulled aside players who were struggling—bubble players on the third or fourth line who might not make the final cut. I had them over to my house or took them out for coffee and gave them some pointers, things to work on to get their game on track. I made sure they knew that I had their backs, and then I did.

Part of being in leadership is getting to know your colleagues and your team. You have to figure out ways to connect with them as individuals, to show that you care about them and their development. When Noah got to be a little older, I was finally able to carve out more time for my teammates and learn about their lives away from the rink: what made them tick, where they came from, what their families were like. Going forward, I always made time for this.

When people know you care about their development, they are more likely to perform and to listen to you as a leader. Once I understood a player, I could help bring the best out of them by touching the right nerve at the right time.

I pulled one of our players aside at her first World Championships in Switzerland. She went on to be a Division 1 standout in the NCAA and now coaches in the U.S. But in Switzerland all those years ago, she was young and immature. She was struggling under the weight of expectations and wasn't handling the pressure very well. I thought she was a terrific player with a lot of upside, and so I told her, "You'll either play on this team for a very long time or have a very short career. I want you to know that I think you're a really good player, but you have to get your head out of your ass."

I know it hurt her in the moment. But she later thanked me for it. We have remained friends through the years. Those conversations suck. But if I hadn't cared about her, I wouldn't have said anything. If I'm being straight with you, it's because I respect you and care about you. Players need to know that you genuinely care about them to be receptive to feedback, whether it's positive or constructive. Though it's hard to hear, constructive feedback is never a bad thing: failure is a part of life, and every single day we make mistakes as human beings. I made them as a leader, too. I gave praise sparingly, perhaps too infrequently. I could be distant, remote. There were times I pushed too hard.

Being in leadership is one of the toughest jobs out there. As a leader, I never let anyone off easy. I held us all accountable, myself included. I was never afraid of being unpopular. Being a captain was often lonely as hell, and I felt constant pressure to be strong, to not make mistakes. I wish I had realized earlier that vulnerability doesn't undercut your authority as a leader, but enhances it. Making mistakes is unavoidable. But being honest and open about those mistakes makes you a better leader. Acting with empathy first, always, makes you a better leader and a better person.

- Take the time to get to know your team. Let them know you have their back, then do.

- Sometimes you lead from the front, sometimes you need to lead from behind.

15.

CHANGE YOUR FATE

We are capable of so much more than we think

No matter what anyone says, you can fight destiny, you can change your fate. I learned this a few years ago when I overcame the worst injury of my career. Had I listened to the first four doctors I saw or ignored what my gut was telling me, that injury would have ended my career. I wouldn't be working with the Leafs right now. I'd be dealing with chronic pain. It's a good thing I'm so goddamn stubborn.

At first blush, the injury seemed pretty innocuous. I was at a Team Canada practice in 2012 when I caught a slapshot from Caroline Ouellette on my left foot. Caro was six feet from me when she let it rip. The puck caught me right on the laces, the only part of the skate with no padding. I was pissed in the moment but that's hockey, shit happens. I tried to skate it off. But the pain persisted.

No damage showed up on X-rays, though, so doctors thought it was a bone bruise, not a fracture. I figured it would slowly heal. For months after, the pain kept lingering. The foot felt okay when it was laced up tight inside my skate but awful in a shoe. When I realized that I was gritting back tears just trying to get through a warm-up on the track, I went and got a CT scan, which combines a series of X-ray images from a bunch of different angles for a more complete picture. The CT showed a non-union fracture of the navicular bone.

Most bones heal, or "unite," completely. In some rare cases, however, a fracture refuses to heal and is called a non-union. The navicular is prone to non-union or delayed fractures because it gets very little blood flow—meaning healing is painfully slow.

It is pretty much the worst bone that an athlete can break. It's the foot's major weight-bearing bone and probably the most important in the lower limb. It plays a big role with speed, direction, and push-off. It's also a rare break. Generally, only athletes tend to fracture it. A lot of doctors initially miss it because the thin break can be hard to see on X-rays and there are few signs of a serious injury, like a deformity or swelling. My only symptom was pain in my foot when I put weight on it. (Note to self: any patient I see presenting with symptoms of a navicular injury is heading straight to the CT.)

I needed to get into a boot cast and give the bone time to heal, but it was an Olympic year. I didn't have time to rehab the injury, and I wasn't willing to miss the Games. So, I decided to hold off and wait until we returned from Sochi.

In the lead-up to the Olympics, I did everything I could to protect my foot. I had plastic skate fenders made to cover the top of my skate. I didn't run or do any impact training. All I could do was swim, cycle, and lift weights. I relied as much as I could on my right leg.

Outside our team, no one knew that I was playing on a broken foot. No mention of it made it into any media coverage, even after our come-from-behind 3–2 overtime win over the U.S. for the gold. Playing through pain wasn't new to me, and I didn't want to make a big deal of it. I'd played with a broken wrist in Turin in '06 and managed to bring home MVP honours along with our gold. But this was so much worse. The national team doctors worked hard to keep my pain and swelling down during games. As soon as the tournament was over, I went straight into an air cast.

When my boot came off two months after Sochi, I knew right away that the bone hadn't healed. A CT confirmed it. In August 2014, I underwent surgery to rebuild the bone.

I was playing for the University of Calgary at the time. I took three months to rehab the foot before getting back onto the ice with the Dinos. I made my return in November of that year. My second game back was at Saskatoon's Rutherford Arena, home to the Huskies. During the game, I made a sharp, tight turn and felt my foot crumple around the screw doctors had implanted to hold the bone together. I collapsed on the ice in pain. When Danielle Goyette, my then coach and former teammate, approached me, I said, "It's over—I'm done."

The first four doctors I saw agreed with my on-ice assessment: I would never play hockey again. The navicular was now in four pieces, the CT showed. These surgeons proposed fusing the navicular to a joint in the middle of my foot. The foot fusion would reduce my pain, but it would also stiffen my foot. I would no longer have the mobility and range of motion I needed to play hockey at a high level.

But I wasn't ready to retire from the game yet. At the time, I was hoping to play for Canada in PyeongChang. After some of the initial, excruciating pain passed, I took back my self-assessment. I was going to play again, no matter what it took. I just needed to find a doctor willing to put the bone back together.

The fifth doctor I saw, Dr. Johnny Lau, proposed a procedure that would graft a bone-tissue implant in my foot to put my navicular back together. Dr. Lau, who operates out of Toronto Western Hospital, treats many of the country's elite athletes. He felt confident that he could get my foot back to 90 percent function. The fusion the first four doctors proposed could only get me to 70 percent. But Dr. Lau's procedure would take much longer to rehab and be infinitely more painful.

In studying medicine, the thing I have come to most appreciate is the magic of the human body. Each patient has their own unique history. Each of us is capable of withstanding far more pain and suffering than we know. Something I also learned first-hand.

In February 2015, I flew to Toronto to undergo reconstructive surgery with Dr. Lau. He began by taking a bone graft from my hip, essentially drilling a chunk of bone from the joint, a procedure that is as painful as it sounds. This was the bone tissue they used to rebuild my navicular. A metal plate and eight screws provide a second layer of protection. When he was done, Dr. Lau told me it was the second worst foot injury he had ever seen.

After surgery, I spent four days in a hotel to recover—until I was well enough to fly back to Calgary. I don't like putting anything unnatural in my body and try to avoid painkillers as much as I can. But I knew that my foot would heal faster if I cut the pain in the first few days, allowing my body to relax and begin the hard work of repairing itself. For the first four days, it was just me and the pain train. All I did was sleep and order room service. I didn't even leave my room.

When I got back to Calgary, I was ready to kick the painkillers and begin my recovery. Dr. Lau was clear with me: I could not put my foot on the ground for four months. If I did, the newly reconstructed bone would collapse and I would likely never walk again. He needn't have worried. The foot felt like mush. I had zero desire to take a step. The thought made my stomach turn.

Looking back, the single most important decision I made for my recovery was asking my friend, confidante, and the best physiologist and neural expert there is—Dr. Syl Corbett—to help me heal and get my conditioning back. Though I had long been one of her many clients, I would need her undivided attention to make this work. She agreed to put her other clients on hold for seven months to work with me six hours a day, five days a week. I was still a carded athlete, so I was getting paid by the national team, thank god, or I never could have afforded it. I kept doing some of my speaking gigs and work with sponsors, and I dipped into my savings to be able to hire Syl and make recovery my full-time job for the next seven months.

The thing I like most about Syl is her ability to be honest, sometimes brutally so. I needed Syl to tell me whether she believed that I would walk and play again. I didn't want her to tell me what she thought I needed to hear. I wanted her to be straight with me, and she was. She told me I was going to play again. I just needed to trust her.

Syl had a plan for my recovery. Post-op day 12, we started training. Syl's theory was: sure, your foot is busted but the rest of you is working just fine. So, we're going to train the rest of you. At first, she helped me stretch and massaged my legs to increase blood flow to my foot. Next, we moved into strength training—lifting weights and working my upper body.

Post-op day 23, Syl put me in the pool. I was quite the sight. I'd put my bathing suit on at home, cover my cast with a garbage bag, and seal it with duct tape. Then I'd pull on my sweats. Syl would drive me to the pool, where I'd just have to pull off my sweats and T-shirt and hop in. The lifeguards stared at me like I was nuts, this swimmer with a garbage bag for a foot. For the next two months I lived in that pool.

Every day, I swam 2,000 metres with a pull buoy between my legs, using just my arms to power me. I hate swimming—I get bored in the water—but Syl was with me for every stroke. I got incredibly fit. When I came back to do fitness testing five months later, I logged the highest VO2 max (the maximum rate of oxygen consumption measured during exercise) of my career. My lungs, my breathing, my strength—all were next level.

Outside of the pool, Syl and I did some pretty odd stuff, if the looks I received were any indication. She would get me to put on a weight vest and then stand behind me on a skateboard. I'd attach bungee cords to my shoulders and drag her up a hill. I did all of this on a knee scooter.

—

Recovering from injury is not a linear process. Sometimes, I would get a little better only to hit a plateau. My recovery would flatten for several days. There were setbacks along the way. It's super common to end up with pain elsewhere as you try to fix an injury. I was relying more heavily on my back, which couldn't take the added strain.

But the hardest part was the mental and emotional toll. My foot injury triggered an existential crisis and led me to question my identity, my purpose in the world. The healing felt completely out of my control. My job was playing hockey, and it had been my job for 20 years. *Would I ever be able to do my job again?* There was so much uncertainty. At that point, I didn't even know if I would ever be able to walk without assistance again.

On top of it, a ton of people suddenly exited my life or stopped believing in me. I was a wounded horse. I'd been playing for Team Canada since I was 15, surrounded by a team of 21 girls and a solid support staff. I felt suddenly alone, alienated from my team and the life I had known. That hard and fast stop felt dizzying, confusing. I felt discarded and abandoned. This same thing happens to all athletes when they retire. Their team moves on. Life moves on. They get forgotten. This is why so many athletes spiral following retirement. For two decades I'd been a leader and on the top line. Suddenly, I realized the team didn't need me anymore. Maybe they didn't want me anymore. That's a brutal, hard truth to face.

—

I believed in my ability to come back, but I didn't know whether the bone would hold. I was full of doubt. I'd never questioned my health before. I have always been strong and fit and able to overcome injury. This was all brand new.

It's in dire moments that you realize just what you are capable of. That period was some of the darkest months of my life. I realized that I had only a handful of people who truly believed in me and who I could count on, no matter what. It was a lonely time. I learned how important it is to be your own best friend and to believe in yourself when no one else does.

I never would have recovered if getting better hadn't been my full-time job. A lot of people don't have that luxury. I was goddamned determined not to have my career cut short by an injury. I wanted to go out on my own terms. I focused on winning each day and on the game plan Syl and I created. Most days, that involved the same four elements: rehab, strength training, the pool, and skills training. Knowing where I was going to be every hour of the day helped keep me focused and on track. You know I love a good list. To aid my recovery, I made sure to get 12 hours of sleep every night. I steered clear of alcohol and sugar. I took supplements and followed a diet to help with bone building. Doing all of this helped keep my mind active and focused on my recovery.

I expected recovery would be painful and lonely. What I didn't anticipate was overwhelming grief. I went through waves of it and felt weighed down. I feared losing my career and my livelihood. I was sick of not being able to walk up the stairs in my house. I hated my crutches. I was in pain. I was so isolated.

Would I recover fully? Would I be welcomed back to the team? Would the injury and the damage to my foot be lasting? If I couldn't play hockey, what was I going to do?

Uncertainty about the future makes rehabbing an injury scary. I just kept reminding myself that there would be the valleys and plateaus. That it was okay not to be okay. I did my best to stay positive. I had to learn to go easy on myself, to cut myself some slack. And when I wasn't okay, I reached out to my people—my family, my friends, my mentors. I asked for help. Syl was there to keep reminding me that it was going to be okay, that I was going to get better, that we were actively working to fix it. She helped me stay calm without taking on my bad energy.

The key for me was acknowledging those feelings, accepting that they lived in my head, and then getting on with the hard work of recovering. I deployed a lot of the strategies that I have outlined in this book. I needed them all.

It was also important for me to remind myself that I was not out of the game. Even though I couldn't play hockey, I could watch it, I could visualize it. I studied video. I studied players. I would sit in my garage, stickhandling for hours. I used Tim Hortons cups and little pylons, and ran through drills. I worked on my shooting from my scooter. I remained in the game, even though I couldn't play it.

In all, it took me four months to walk again, five months to skate again, and a year to run again. I had terrible days. Some mornings, I woke in excruciating pain. Getting back my foot function took everything I had. It tested me in every single way. But I was able to return to the ice and, more importantly, to feel that I could have a long life after hockey with a relatively healthy foot.

Today, I am back to running, cycling, and training normally. I can skate for hours in my role with the Toronto Maple Leafs. My foot aches after a long skate, and I think I'm developing arthritis in it. But there were countless days I wasn't sure I'd be able to do any of this. I train every day to strengthen my foot so that I'll have my foot health for the rest of my life, and I won't be limited by it. That injury will not stop me from living the life I want to live. There are too many great things I still want to do.

Looking back, when I was sitting in those doctors' offices with my navicular bone in four parts, I see that I had a choice. I could choose a path where I'd recover 70 percent function and accept that my career was over. Or I could choose to find out how much I was capable of. I chose to ignore the prognoses for a limited recovery. Deep down, I believed that more was possible, that I could get my foot and body back to game shape.

There were days during those long months of recovery when those beliefs wavered or even felt laughable. Getting back on the ice took absolutely everything I had. The journey showed me that we are capable of doing and achieving so much more than we think. It made me see that the insecurities and fears and all the other limits we create inside our heads are often the only things keeping us stuck in a life that is smaller than we deserve. It reminded me why I surround myself with people like Syl Corbett, Andy O'Brien, and Darryl Belfry, fellow dreamers who keep me thinking big, who know that the world is full of possibilities, who challenge me to think outside the box and try things that have never been done before. Like me, they know that more is always possible. The process also opened my eyes to a new level of pain and suffering and to what being a patient is really like. It solidified my desire to go to medical school. I was living proof of the hope and possibility of medicine. I had changed my fate.

- Each of us is capable of battling through so much more than we know.

- Acknowledge and accept the fears that live inside our heads. Then get on with the work that needs to be done.

16.

KIDS ARE OUR TRUTH TELLERS

Kids will change you—whether you're ready or not

I never wanted to keep anything from Noah. But I wavered once.

When he was in grade four, his dad, Tomas Pacina, and I briefly debated whether or not to tell him that I hadn't been the one who gave birth to him. I was scared—of hurting Noah.

When I was growing up, it was still pretty rare to tell adopted kids this key fact about them. There's been a sea change since. These days, experts tell parents to disclose the story of a child's adoption ideally from a young age, so the child grows up feeling they have an honest understanding of their origins.

With Noah, we knew that suddenly learning about his birth mother would have been a shock and a lot to handle all at once had we let him believe one thing his entire life. To tell him, we eased into it, showing Noah photos of his birth mom holding him in the neonatal intensive care unit. He spent his first six weeks in the NICU, having arrived three months premature. We read him books about adoption, explaining it to him bit by bit, using language he could understand. This process ended up being more for us, because Noah got it right away.

Of course, once he learned about her, Noah was keen to meet his birth mother. Telling Noah that I didn't carry him had been a huge, scary step for me. Now this . . . as hard as it is to admit, I felt threatened. I was gripped by an irrational fear that Noah would reject me once he met his birth mother. That he would run to her and say, "This is the mom I've always wanted." That he would turn to me and say, "You're not my *real* mom."

We arranged to meet Noah's birth mom at the neighbourhood pool so she could watch him swim, then join us in the water. When we introduced the two of them, Noah looked up at her and said "Hi" in a small voice. Then he ran to me, grabbing my leg, something he hadn't done in a few years. Feeling his hot little hands gripping my thighs, I realized that I was still who he turned to when he was unsure or scared. I was still his safe place.

Kids are so pure and beautiful. It doesn't matter whether you give birth to them or not, there is no difference in the way you love them—or the way they love you. Later I came to realize that by respecting Noah's history, I was respecting him. I was helping him build his story. And I was normalizing his adoption. In retrospect, I think by not avoiding it or letting it become this big, scary thing, the transition felt natural and easy for all of us. This is just one of many lessons Noah has taught me.

The first time I held Noah, I thought, *This beautiful, tiny human is going to forever change me.* Boy, did he ever. Noah came into this world weighing a whopping one pound, 10 ounces. Lying flat, he was the length of my hand. I was thrilled, but man, it was a lot coming at me all at once. A baby can be hard to manage as a new mom and Noah was a very, very sick little guy. I was 21, a first-year science student at the University of Calgary. I was back from Sydney where I had competed for Canada in softball at the 2000 Summer Olympics, and we were just two years out from the Salt Lake Winter Games.

When I was solely an athlete, my time was my own. I was selfish with it, dedicating it to improving my game, resting, working out. Suddenly, my time belonged to someone else. In this, I wasn't any different from any other first-time parent. As soon as your first child is born, your focus is given over to another being, to feeding them, clothing them, bathing them, reading to them, keeping them alive, warm, healthy, safe. Instead of studying video, I spent every free moment I had doing laundry, picking up toys, rocking my son, wandering the darkened house with him. My energy became an issue because Noah didn't really sleep for the first year. He was in pain, he had trouble eating and keeping food down, he was up every couple hours. I had always been rigid about getting at least 10 hours of sleep each night. I had to learn to function on very little sleep. I didn't have a choice.

It was the best thing for me. Athletes are susceptible to the "disease of me." We get caught up in what *we* want, what *we* need to perform. Getting outside of that bubble, being part of something larger than yourself, reminds you that there are bigger things in life. It gives you a lot more perspective.

Looking back, every one of my teammates who had kids returned to the game following their child's birth a better athlete. Something profound changes in you. You have a higher pain tolerance. You become tougher. You can sustain effort longer. You become more disciplined, more focused. You are better able to respond to challenges. You just become resilient. My former teammate Cheryl Pounder may have said it best: "I can pass a watermelon through my vagina. This beep test has nothing on that."

It didn't surprise me at all when Serena Williams won four Grand Slam tennis finals starting at 10 months postpartum. Or when tennis star Kim Clijsters won the 2009 U.S. Open as a brand-new mom. Or when Paula Radcliffe, arguably the greatest women's marathoner of all time, won the New York City Marathon in 2007 in her return to the sport after giving birth to a daughter.

I can't tell you how it happens. Maybe it's because you have no other choice. This little bean that's stuck in your arms all day and night is relying on you, 100 percent. Becoming a parent opens up your world and makes the challenges you face on the ice not seem as huge as they once did. Being a parent helped me gain more control of my emotions on the ice. Back when I was 19, I had focused solely on winning. When things went wrong, my emotions bubbled over, disproportionately. Now, I had a little guy waiting for me at home who needed me. Getting tripped or receiving a cheap shot suddenly felt a lot less important. Pushing through another couple wind sprints when my legs were telling me they were dead, that was nothing after staying up night after night with a baby in pain. Motherhood showed me just how much I was capable of. It deepened my inner fortitude and taught me entirely new lessons in commitment, sacrifice, perseverance.

Having Noah also changed how I interacted with my teammates. He opened up my heart. I became a bit more empathetic, more understanding, especially of the younger players. The downside was, I wasn't able to spend my free time with them, the way I used to. I had to rush home from practice to care for my baby.

During the day, Noah napped rink-side in his bassinet. Tomas was coaching my team, the Calgary Oval X-Treme of the NWHL. While we skated, an injured player or a therapist watched him. My teammates were amazing. They were so excited to have a little baby around, and a lot of them babysat for me. They loved it when I brought Noah into the dressing room. I was fortunate to have great support. My sister, Jane, helped out a ton. So did my mom and dad. When Noah got a bit older, we hired a nanny, "Grandma Janice," as he called her. She took care of Noah along with her grandson, Isaac, who remains Noah's best friend to this day.

Becoming Noah's mom showed me how much kids can teach us. He changed me in every single way. We can all get stuck on what happened at work, and after a rough day of frustrations and deadlines and meetings, the last thing you feel like doing is getting down on your knees to play LEGO or Thomas the Train. (Try doing that after getting bag skated.) The thing is, kids are deeply intuitive. They notice a lot more than we realize. It took me a while, but I came to see that Noah picked up on my stresses and frustrations. He could see when I was distracted with him.

Once, Noah wanted me to play trains with him. I was watching hockey at the time and kept telling him, "In a minute, in a minute." I saw his shoulders slump when he realized I wasn't coming.

Then he turned around and started playing all by himself. He looked so sad, so lonely. I remember thinking to myself, *Hayley, what the hell are you doing? Hockey can wait.*

I eventually realized that I was often distracted even when I was spending time with him. I was thinking about hockey or training, or some problem on the team. I wasn't present. And he noticed—long before I figured it out—and it was hurting him.

Your kids don't care what you do for a living. They don't want to know what happened at the office. The only thing that matters to them is that when you walk through the front door, you are present. That nothing matters more to you than them. When I obsessed over hockey, I was signalling to Noah that the game was number one in my heart. I had to learn real fast to leave my shit behind at the rink.

I set up some firm boundaries. When I came into the house I left hockey behind and was fully present and engaged. We'd play together before sitting down to eat. Before bed, I bathed Noah and read to him. Our time together became sacred. It was a no-hockey, no-stress zone. Once he went to sleep, I could go back to focusing on other things.

A lot of women feel guilty when they're away from their families and their kids. I didn't ever wrestle with those feelings. Noah always understood that sometimes Mom would be gone, but Mom was always going to come back. And when Mom was back, Mom was fully present. I would always have time for Noah. Being engaged and not distracted when I was with him made it a lot easier to be away.

Noah also helped knock me back down to earth. He never cared that I was a hockey player. He has no interest in the game.

He hates it. I think it's because when he saw Mom and Dad stressing out, it was because of hockey. In Vancouver, he spent the Olympic final with his nose buried in a *Harry Potter* book. I never pushed him to play. I enrolled him in gymnastics instead. He swam competitively into his teens. He joined the cadets. But he had no interest in hockey, and I was just fine with that. Our kids are perfect the way they are. They have their own dreams. Our job is to help them pursue them.

Parenting has had the largest impact in showing me the power of people, but kids aren't the only ones who change our lives forever. I'm incredibly lucky to have had so many coaches who became important parts of my life, who became mentors and friends. People I could turn to in moments of doubt, about anything. They've changed my life immeasurably. And when something happens and someone we love is in danger, the threat of no longer having them around is sobering. In 2007, Wally Kozak had a massive heart attack while he was on the ice coaching a women's game in Strathmore, Alberta. Wally remains one of the best coaches I ever had. His hockey IQ is unmatched. But more than that, he is a father figure to me. Since I was a teenager, he has been with me every step of the way. He has helped me cope when my anxiety over losing or not scoring turned the fire blazing inside me inward.

The night Wally had his heart attack, several of my teammates with medical training—including Kari Colpitts and Corinne Swirsky, who train Calgary police officers—happened to be on the ice. They hauled out the rink's portable defibrillator—a smaller version of the electrical paddles used in emergency rooms—and got to work. I've never been more thankful that women weren't paid to play hockey in that league, and that there were players on the ice who had chosen emergency response careers.

With a cardiac arrest, every second counts. If you can restore the heart's rhythm within four minutes, most people can survive a heart attack with no permanent damage. For every minute beyond that, the risk of mortality rises by 10 percent. So does the likelihood of brain damage. After about 10 minutes, death is virtually certain. From the time he collapsed to the time he arrived at the hospital, my friends and EMS had defibrillated Wally 13 times combined.

I was on a different ice surface that night, with a bunch of national team players in Calgary. When word reached me, I left the ice, stripped out of my equipment, and raced to the hospital without showering. When I got there, doctors had cooled Wally's body to try to prevent brain damage. His wife, Trudy, told me she didn't know if he was going to make it. Doctors, I learned later, had given Wally a 5 percent chance of survival.

Wally underwent quadruple bypass surgery and spent the next month in a coma. They weren't sure if he would recognize his family members when he woke up. One afternoon, I was sitting with him in the hospital after practice, and he opened his eyes and said, "Wick, how you doin'?" Seconds after coming out of that coma, he wanted to start talking hockey. Trudy just laughed.

The fact that Wally had to be defibrillated so many times and was so ill was sobering. I think we look at our parents as sort of invincible. The thought of Wally exiting my life so early and so suddenly was incredibly painful. While he was in a coma, I spent every day in hospital, watching over him. Being there, seeing him hooked up to machines keeping him alive, reminded me of what is really important. The medals and awards I have won are nothing compared with the people dear to me. They are my power. Ever since then, I have tried to make relationships my number one priority.

I interact with thousands of people every year, but there are only a handful of people I make time for religiously. My family and a tight-knit group of friends keep me humble and grounded and connected to my roots. They fill me up, give me energy, and are positive and fun to be around. They make me a bigger and better version of myself.

We all need outlets, people we trust who can allow us to vent, who give us the space and support to step outside the rink, the office, the hospital, or wherever else, so we can regain some perspective. We gain so much from the companionship, connection, and love we get from the people dear to us. People are the power in our lives; they keep us going. They remind us of what is important.

When I was writing this book, Noah was studying art and military history at the University of Victoria. He has passions that are all his own. We spend a ton of time together in museums and galleries; we go antiquing together and check out vintage cars (well, we do when there's no pandemic!). He's a seeker and a true original.

Two years ago, he won a leadership award for leading a unit of 20 boys with behavioural and intellectual challenges. He stayed an extra year in cadets to be able to work with them. It was cool to see him pick up that award, decked out in his dress uniform.

The tables were turned: usually it's him watching me accept an award. That day, I was just another face in the crowd. I'm probably the most laid-back parent there is, a sharp contrast to who I am as an athlete.

Noah made me a better player and a better person. He taught me patience and introduced me to new perspectives. He made me less selfish. He showed me what is really important in life. He taught me to be vulnerable. With him, I have felt the purest joy. He is without question the light of my life.

- Becoming a parent opens up your world and makes the challenges you face seem so much smaller.
- People are the power in our lives; they keep us going.

17.

LEAVING A LEGACY

Leave the game better than you found it

The first time I met Steve Montador, he walked into the gym wearing two different-coloured dress socks. He looked like he'd been having a pretty good time the night before. This was sometime in 2002; Monty was a teammate of Marty Gélinas, my training buddy, and Marty had invited Monty to join us for a lift. After we teased Monty about his socks, we got to work.

Monty was a big guy and super strong—he easily benched over 300 pounds. Yet he had an innocence about him, a stark contrast to his physique. With his gap-toothed grin and open personality, he seemed like a boy in a man's body.

We became fast friends, training together and skating during summers. One summer night, Monty and I were at a barbecue at Marty's house to celebrate the hard work we'd been putting in at the gym. Our families were all out of town so it was just the three of us, sipping beer, jawing about hockey, cracking jokes. Moments like those were some of the best times of my career.

When I was with Monty, there were always a lot of laughs and ridiculous antics. He was totally unpredictable. As we got closer, though, I noticed there were ups and downs, too. We each had our struggles and started opening up to one another about them.

Shortly after that barbecue, Monty seemed to disappear for a while. The next time I saw him, he pulled me aside. He confided that he was battling some demons. He was getting help and wanted to let me know what was going on. I told him I was proud of him and was always there if he needed me. I knew he lived life pretty fast, but at the time, I didn't know many details. I didn't know then that those demons would continue to haunt him.

A couple years later, Marty was traded to Florida. Another trade saw Monty following Marty there. I had just started working with Andy O'Brien, Florida's trainer at the time, and so was able to see the both of them on my trips down. Monty seemed to gain confidence in the Sunshine State. He remained committed to his conditioning and to living a healthy lifestyle. He was more talented than any of us realized.

We kept up over the years, usually when we both happened to be in Toronto. We'd meet for a workout at U of T or grab lunch. In 2011, one of my closest friends was struggling with addiction. I was afraid he might hurt himself. The first person I called was Monty. Right away, he helped guide me to a top treatment centre and arranged for my friend to go there at no cost. Monty helped save his life. That's who he was. He had a heart of gold. My friend has been sober five years now.

Then in 2012, when Monty was playing for Chicago, he suffered a debilitating concussion that kept him off the ice for a year. He was struggling to feel good, he told me; he was depressed. He was reading a lot of research about the impact of head injuries. I think that he knew his hockey career was over, that he was scared of what his future might look like. I could see the pain in his eyes. Concussions forced him to walk away from the game shortly after.

I've never been formally diagnosed with a concussion. But I know I've had at least one serious brain injury. It happened in 2008 when I was playing professional men's hockey in Sweden. I'd worked out a deal with my team, Eskilstuna Linden, so that I could keep my commitments to Team Canada. When I went to Lake Placid for the Four Nations Cup that winter, I took a bad hit in the final and tore my MCL, one of the ligaments that help stabilize the knee joint. I was crushed—knee injuries don't heal quickly. I rushed through a two-week rehab in Toronto before returning to Sweden to finish recuperating. I gave myself 10 days. I knew I should've taken longer to heal, but I was under a ton of stress. I was the only one bringing in money for my family. The team's ownership was paying me to play, and there I go and get hurt while I was seconded to another team. I felt terrible and didn't think Eskilstuna would be willing to invest in a lengthy rehabilitation. I was also the only woman playing at that level: so many people wanted to see me fail, and I didn't want to give them the satisfaction.

My coach at the time was Mattias Karlin, who'd been a fantastic player in his day. He was drafted by Boston in the third round and played for Modo in the Swedish first division. He was very understanding of the injury, more understanding than I was. He didn't want to push me. He knew I was tough. I'll never forget what he said when I told him I was ready to play: "Hayley, I know that physically you look ready, but mentally you need more time. There's the physical rehab and then there's the mental rehab."

As it turned out, Mattias was dead right. Mentally, I wasn't ready to return to the men's game. I needed time in practice to get used to the hitting again and regain a feel for the pacing. Mattias wanted me to sit and watch the first 10 minutes of the next game before I went in. I didn't love the idea—when you're sitting, you get cold. You're not engaged. I didn't think sitting and watching for 10 minutes before being thrown into the play was a great plan, but I wanted back in so bad that I agreed to it. Halfway through the first period, I got the nod.

A number of things went wrong. I was on the wing, a position I wasn't used to. I felt cold and out of place. I wasn't fully present. In hockey, whenever you aren't present, you put yourself at risk. When we were clearing the zone, my defenceman threw me a suicide pass. My body was moving up ice, but my head was turned back towards the puck. I could feel the check coming. The guy drilled me from about 10 feet, hitting me with such force that he ended up shearing off a piece of my vertebrae, though I didn't know that until later.

Fortunately, I was near our bench. The trainer opened the door and one of the guys grabbed me by the pants and lifted me in. I immediately felt sick to my stomach. I blacked out for a second. I tried to be cool. I knew everyone was looking at me, thinking, *Holy shit. She just got hit so hard.*

In the intermission, Mattias came over to me. "Are you okay? That was a horrible hit." I said, "Yeah, I'm good." Then I ducked into my own dressing room and threw up. I took a couple Advils and went back to the team room. I told them I was ready to finish the game. In reality, I was anything but. I'm not proud of that decision. Not at all. At the time, it felt like a matter of survival. I didn't want to lose my career. I didn't want people to say I couldn't handle it. I think a lot of players suffering from concussions feel that way—they're scared that if they say they aren't okay, their careers will end. I know Monty had that fear. So, I faked it.

For the next three weeks, I suffered. It took everything I had to wake up and take Noah to school. I would spend the rest of the day in a dark house, drinking tea or coffee. Light hurt my head, my eyes. Eventually, I recovered and had no lingering, long-term effects. I got lucky. I was spared. Many of my friends, like Monty, were not.

Monty and I had a special bond. I was a pro athlete and understood the hockey world. At the same time, because I was a woman—I wasn't technically one of the guys—I think he felt comfortable with me, that he could be real with me. About a week before he died, Monty's picture popped into my social media feed. It was almost like a sign. Something told me to check in. I texted a quick "Hey—how are ya?"—but never heard back.

A few days later I was preparing for an awards ceremony when my phone wouldn't stop buzzing. When I glanced down, my heart sank. A text reading "Did you hear about Monty?" was across my screen. I knew in that instant he was gone. I felt sick and bolted from the room. Marty called me 10 seconds later in shock. When I got hold of Andy, he told me that Monty had been in the gym the week before and seemed to be okay, but that something had him worried.

The hardest time for any athlete is the day it's finally over. Up to that moment you were a valuable commodity to the team, the league, and the sponsors, and you were treated that way. Overnight, your value goes down and they drop you. I have had teammates who were told, "Thanks, but we don't want you anymore." Guys have told me stories of being involved in conversations about playoff runs in one instant and being handed a garbage bag with their stuff and told goodbye in the next.

A lot of NHLers I know are lucky if they've finished high school or done some post-secondary education. It is almost impossible to plan and pursue other career options while you are playing 82 games a season. It's a grind. The travel and fatigue are unrelenting. Mentally, you're focused on recovering from the game and performing the next day. When those guys retire, a lot of them are in their early 30s. They have a lot of living left to do. A lot of them end up feeling pretty lost. I know Monty did.

He'd spent 10 years in the NHL. He was just 35 and three years out of the game when he died at his home in Ontario. Four days after his death, his ex-girlfriend gave birth to his first child, a son. His cause of death has never been made public, but his post-mortem showed chronic traumatic encephalopathy (CTE) in his brain, which can be attributed to the brain injuries he suffered playing hockey.

Monty was one of my dearest friends. He was a beautiful, intelligent soul. When he was playing a season in the KHL, he'd sign off his emails to me with "From Russia with love." His death left me determined to make hockey safer and more supportive. A few years ago, I pledged to donate my brain to the Veterans Affairs–Boston University–Concussion Legacy Foundation Brain Bank after my death to support the research and treatment of CTE. It was a first step towards that goal.

It's funny, but in my role with the Leafs, I find myself having the same kinds of conversations with young players that I used to have with Monty. I know medicine and the human body. I have been through injury and have fought back from it. I think some players see me the way Monty did and feel able to open up in ways they might not be able to with a male coach. I'm always willing to lend an ear. I want to help them. I hope I might be able to help in ways that I wasn't able to help Monty.

For me, planning for life after hockey also meant thinking about the kind of legacy that I wanted to leave behind after my retirement from the game. No matter what you do for a living, I think it's important to always look for ways to give back. To make our sports, industries, and the world a better place for those who come after us. That might mean mentoring someone, getting involved in a professional association, or helping out a young colleague who seems to be struggling.

The first time someone asked me what I wanted to do for my sport, I was caught totally unprepared for the question. It was during the 2000 Olympic Games in Sydney, where I was playing softball for Team Canada. One morning, I was walking through the athletes' village when a bunch of South African athletes came running up behind me, shouting: "Madiba! Madiba is coming." One of them turned to me and said, "Do you want to meet Nelson Mandela?" I said, "Oh my god, yeah."

His face lined and deeply weathered, Mandela was a lot taller and skinnier than he appeared in pictures and on TV. He was wearing a floral button-up shirt. He led us—six other athletes and me—into an empty room where we sat down. He talked to us about the power of sport to bring unity and peace. Then he asked each of us, "What will you do to leave your sport and the world better than you found it?" He had a calm but wilful aura. I didn't have much of an answer for him. It was embarrassing. Until that point I'd been focusing on getting all I could out of sports. In challenging me this way, Mandela helped me see that I needed to think about what I could give back. As athletes, we have been given so much. The way I see it, it's on us to pay it forward, to inspire and mentor the generation coming up behind us.

You know that saying, "You have to see it to be it"? Back when I was growing up, I didn't know many other girls who played hockey, and I didn't see any women playing professionally. I didn't have any role models. I didn't see it. Because it didn't exist. So, after the 2010 Olympics in Vancouver, I decided that I wanted to help promote the women's game, particularly in British Columbia, where it was less developed than in other parts of Canada. That summer I launched an international hockey festival in Burnaby. These days, it's officially known as the Canadian Tire Wickenheiser World Female Hockey Festival and it takes place in Calgary. But everyone just calls it "WickFest." We've since expanded the tournament to Surrey, B.C., and have plans to expand into eastern Canada in the coming years. All the money we earn goes to Right to Play and Jumpstart, charities that help provide equal access for kids to get involved in sports.

We run the three-day event as a professional and personal development weekend for girls in hockey. Between games, the girls take sessions in everything from fitness to nutrition to mental wellness and budgeting. We bring in leaders like Prime Minister Justin Trudeau, female role models like astronaut Roberta Bondar, and NHLers like Andrew Ference, Trevor Linden, and Mason Raymond. Hockey is meant to be secondary; I want to teach the girls how to be a complete athlete and to empower and develop them as people, not just players.

I've mentioned earlier about how, when the COVID-19 pandemic broke out, I put my public profile to good use by launching a drive for personal protective equipment for health care workers. People on social media sometimes harp on me to shut up and stick to hockey. But I think they're wrong. Athletes have profiles and status in this world; we have opportunities to influence social change. What good are our public profiles if we don't use them to help others?

Life can be short. I saw that when Monty died. I see it in the ER all the time. In the trauma bay, I have the honour of treating people on the worst day of their lives. I have also witnessed medical miracles there. Whenever I leave the hospital, I feel full of energy; I feel so alive. It's like I'm exhausted but wired at the same time. Spending time there has helped me understand the reason we are here: to serve, to help others, to give back. I don't know that I fully understood that while I was still in the game.

I wish I could give Mandela my answer now.

- No matter what you do for a living, it's important to look for ways to give back.
- Try to leave your game, your industry, your world a little bit better than when you found it.

18.

GO SLOW TO GO FAST

Do things as well as possible rather than as fast as possible

The last Olympic game I played was probably the most exciting of my career. But it didn't start off that way.

During warm-up at Sochi's Bolshoy Ice Dome in February 2014, I couldn't shake the sadness from my legs. I didn't yet know if this would be my last Olympic game, but it was a possibility. I'd been with Team Canada for 20 years and couldn't ignore that I was no longer among the younger players on the team. Time comes for us all. The day that someone would finally tell me that I couldn't play anymore was on the horizon. That knowledge hurt like hell.

I was already feeling emotional on my way out to the ice when I looked up and saw Noah. He was hanging over the railing, calling to me. He was 14 years old, and this was his fourth Olympics.

It was the first time he ever painted his face in white and red, and he was holding a sign. "Good luck," he yelled down to me. "I'm proud of you."

I got teary-eyed. I had to take a few minutes to compose myself. For his whole life I'd been dragging Noah to rinks all over the world, and he always found things to do other than watch the games. In that moment, I realized that he got it—how important this game was to me.

For most of the game, the Americans were dominating us. They were forechecking better, defending better. They were playing as a unit. We were running around, one-manning it, working too hard. It was chaotic, ugly hockey. "Silver's gonna look really good on you," one American heckled at the faceoff circle.

My first Olympic outing in Nagano had ended in heartbreak, with a gutting loss to Team USA. It was looking like my final Winter Games might wrap the same way. The hockey gods, however, had other plans.

At the end of the third, we were trailing the U.S., 2–0. With just 3:26 remaining, Brianne Jenner sliced through the American defence, firing a fluttering, harmless-looking shot. It was heading several feet wide of the goal, then bounced off an American knee and into the back of the net.

I looked over at Kevin Dineen, our head coach. We both nodded. A two-goal lead is the most dangerous in hockey. Teams start to ease their foot off the gas. When the trailing team cuts the lead by half, the leading team often panics. That's exactly what happened on that ice. When we got that goal, the Americans knew we were coming: our energy spiked and we kept the pressure on, while they panicked.

My friend Ceilidh, who was there with my family, was keeping a close eye on both benches. In that moment you could feel the energy on the American bench change, she says. It became frenetic. Team USA's coaches started pacing up and down. Their players kept standing up, then sitting down; grabbing water bottles, then putting them down. A perfect calm had descended on our bench. You could have rested a plank on us, we were so still.

Heart and desire are always the strongest part of the Canadian game, Anatoly Tarasov, the great Red Army coach, once said: Canadians "battle with the ferocity and intensity of a cornered animal." And so it was in Sochi.

When the clock ticked down to 1:35, we called a timeout to plan our final assault. We pulled goaltender Shannon Szabados for an extra attacker.

Our pressure ramped up even more, but we lost a key draw in the U.S.'s end. One of the linesmen got tangled up with our defender and the puck found the blade of an American who fired it at our open net from her own blue line. For a few seconds, it looked as if they'd clinched the game. It took *forever* for the puck to cross the ice before clanging harmlessly off the post. We were still alive with 1:25 left to play.

It's a sign, I remember thinking. *We're going to win this thing.*

With less than a minute to go, Rebecca Johnston, a Cornell graduate from Sudbury, Ontario, known as "Johnny," threw a blind pass out front. It bounced off the side of the U.S. net and to Marie-Philip Poulin, who punched it past the U.S. tender, Jessie Vetter. With just 54.6 seconds left on the clock, we were right back where we started: a 0–0 ballgame.

There was a huge buzz in the dressing room when we came in for a final break before overtime. Our leadership group addressed the team: we told them we had the best goaltender in the world in Szabby and that we were well prepared for OT. The overtime period would be played four on four, in keeping with international rules. We had spent a lot of time practising for this very scenario. The plan was to relentlessly press the Americans, force them to make mistakes. "Safe is death," we said. We were sending three high, leaving one on D, rather than playing two plus two.

We needed to play as a unit, making short, tight passes, like the old Soviet squads under Tarasov. The puck can move faster in a pass than any human could ever skate.

Augustus, the first Roman emperor, had a philosophy he called *festina lente*—to "make haste slowly." He didn't mean that people should move at a snail's pace, but rather that they should execute things as well as possible instead of as fast as possible. Speed can come not from being rushed but from a series of small, well-executed steps.

We are steeped in a culture of speed, so much so that it can feel at times like we're living in fast-forward. This conditions us to think that slow means lazy. Or that slow means indecisive. Or that slows means stupid. That if we don't rush, we'll be left in the dust. Reject that thinking. Hockey's greatest players have the ability to slow the game down, twisting their defenders into a pretzel, lulling them, before taking off with lightning speed.

Whether you're an entrepreneur, a scientist, or an athlete, building a successful company, career, or team is about more than velocity. It's about seeding success long before you reap the rewards of your labour. It's about balancing urgency with caution. It's about moving slowly enough to make the needed fixes as they come up. Otherwise, you have to keep going back and repairing mistakes. That'll really slow you down.

Six minutes into OT, the U.S. was awarded a power play. With the four-on-three advantage, it seemed likely the Americans could correct their third period meltdown. But six seconds into the kill, Szabby made a sweet glove save on a shot from the point. Jocelyne Lamoureux—one of a pair of dual American-Canadian twins raised in and playing for the U.S.—was called for a controversial slash. Lamoureux had hit Szabados on the pad with her stick, trying to jar the puck loose as the whistle went. It's not a call you see often in a final. But Lamoureux had been cautioned for it earlier in the game. This gave us huge momentum.

It reminded me of something I'd witnessed two years prior at the London Olympics. A similar situation had played out when Canada met the U.S. in the soccer semi-finals. In the 76th minute, Canadian goalkeeper Erin McLeod was called for holding the ball for more than six seconds. Team USA got a free kick that led to a goal by Megan Rapinoe and an overtime gold to the U.S.

Sometimes you get a feeling about a game, and watching that one, I had felt the game slipping away from Canada. I saw the red, white, and blue machine coming for them. They smelled blood in the water. I had felt the impending doom. You resign yourself to the fact that there is only so much you can do and only so much time left. I think that kind of knowing comes from experience; I've been in that same spot.

In London, the U.S. capitalized on Canada's frustration and anger about the late penalty. I knew we could do the same that night in Sochi, capitalizing on their frustration with the call on Lamoureux as we went three on three.

A minute and a half into the three on three, I grabbed a loose puck on a bad American line change and took off on a clear, 170-foot breakaway. Hilary Knight, probably the best American power forward of her generation, was at my heels. The problem was, I'd got caught out there too long. I had no legs.

Knight's a smart player. On any other night, she would have known she could easily catch me. The race wasn't even a contest— she pulled even with me before I got to their blue line. I think the stress of overtime and anger generated by the late penalty converged, causing her to slip up.

When stress makes you feel angry, afraid, or threatened, your limbic system floods your body with hormones. The "fight or flight" response evolved as a survival mechanism, enabling us to act quickly. But when your body's reaction to stressors overpowers your mind, you can't think straight. I can't climb inside Knight's mind, but I know the intense stress of sudden-death overtime in an Olympic final. I could see that the plan we'd hashed out in the locker room before OT was working—the relentless pressure we had heaped on the U.S. was causing them to crack. As Knight was pulling even with me, she clipped me, sending me crashing to the ice.

The ref lifted her arm as I fell. But she never pointed to centre ice. I skated over to ask why she wasn't awarding me a penalty shot. She stopped me. "You're going four on three," she said. Knight was being penalized for cross-checking. International rules don't let teams skate three on two, so the ref was putting one of our players back on the ice. *Even better*, I thought. I'm not great on the penalty shot. This gave me a few minutes to get my wind back.

Just before the eight-minute mark, Poulin fired a slapshot that was blocked by an American defender. That was the last time Team USA touched the puck that night.

On that power play we were in total sync, dangling the puck, faking shots, going slow to go fast. All four of us touched the disc at least twice, nobody for more than a second or two. We made nine passes between us. The 10th went to Poulin.

Just before the puck got to Poulin, I slid in front of Vetter for the screen. Poulin buried the biscuit for her second goal of the night, giving Canada our fourth straight and, let's face it, most improbable gold medal.

It was the most spectacular comeback I had ever been part of. We scored two goals in the last three and a half minutes of regulation to get us to overtime, then a fourth and final goal to give us the gold over our archrivals. Our opponents expectedly had another opinion. "We had them at the end," U.S. captain Meghan Duggan told NBC's Pierre McGuire after the game. "A couple of bounces went their way and they tied it up." No disrespect to Meghan, but chalking up that comeback to a couple lucky bounces was quite the understatement. Maybe I would feel the same way if I had been on the other side—but from where I was skating, we won by a late burst of total execution, doing everything as well as we possibly could. As Augustus said, you gotta go slow to go fast.

When I got to my stall after the medals were handed out, I sat there watching the girls celebrate. I was too tired, too emotional to join in. The Sochi journey had been a brutal slog, with coaching changes, leadership changes, a horrific injury. The road to Sochi brought back a lot of lessons from earlier in my career— to harness the doubt, to consider pressure as a privilege, to trust in my preparation—and a couple new ones as well.

All you can hope for in hockey is a few moments of perfection every now and again. Those moments belong to you. I was lucky. Not everyone gets to bid farewell to their Olympic journey on such a high note. That final was one of the best games I've ever played. I logged 36 minutes, more than anyone else, and I was tied for the most points for Canada that Olympic tournament.

I sat in my stall in my pants and skates, soaked in sweat, reflecting on the years that had led to this moment.

Hockey had been my first true love. I changed in boiler rooms and bathroom stalls. I put my body through hell and back. I moved across the world in pursuit of perfection. I studied the best the game had and practised their every move. The game gave me both joy and pain. But I wouldn't have it any other way.

That night, I was lucky for another reason, too. I'd had an awful, shitty, no good year. We had lost two-thirds of our games in the run-up to Sochi. I had dealt with pain and fatigue and a terrible foot injury. We underwent a leadership change, a coaching change, and a complete culture overhaul within our team. In the months leading up to the Games, I was haunted by an intense fear of failure—we *had* to win. We had to find a way. All of that weighed on me like a 1,000-pound gorilla. So when I saw the puck slide into the net in OT, it felt like someone had come down from the roof of the rink and lifted all that weight from my shoulders. I felt light as a feather.

—

Throughout this incredible journey, the one thing I have always believed is that I have zero limitations. You are no different from me. If you take one thing from this book, let that be it. You are the author of your fate. Nothing can limit you, except your fears.

Take the road less travelled. Carve your own path. Make an impact. Be kind. Seek out the good. Believe in yourself. Be relentless. Be unbowed.

- Do things as well as possible, not as fast as possible.
- Speed comes from a series of small, well-executed steps.

ACKNOWLEDGMENTS

Countless people have had an impact on me and my game, and they all share in my successes. I'd like to thank just a few.

My family: my mom, Marilyn, and my dad, Tom, believed that anything a boy could do, a girl could, too. My mom fought tooth and nail for my right to play the game. My parents did everything they could to support my dreams. They sacrificed everything to put my brother, sister, and me in hockey and keep us there. For a while, it felt like every spare dime they had was going to pay for hockey camp or a new stick. My brother, Ross, and my sister, Jane, who sometimes had to live in the shadow of my career, have always been my greatest supporters and right there with me every step of the way.

My beautiful son, Noah, deserves my four gold medals for putting up with me for the last 20 years. He's shared in the game's highs. But he is all too aware of the stresses, the anxiety, and the enormous emotional toll the game has taken on us both. Noah is wise beyond his years and has made me a better player and person.

I've had incredible people around me throughout the years, and my career wouldn't have gotten to where it did without them. Wally Kozak has been a teacher and a father figure to me. He is also one of the best coaches I ever had. Wally was someone I turned to when I needed help. He taught me that there is more to life than hockey and has always had my back.

Bob Clarke is a great friend and mentor. Early on in my hockey career, Bob taught me that hockey is a game that cannot be played without three things: skill, discipline, and passion. He invited me to two Philadelphia Flyers camps—two of the most unforgettable experiences of my entire career.

My best friend Dr. Syl Corbett is brilliant trainer and one of the best athletes I know. I credit Syl with every gold medal I have won in the last decade. She has kept me at the top of my game. She has also been a rock for me and seen me through some really hard times.

My trainer Andy O'Brien has helped me expand my physical capacity and taught me to work smarter, not harder. Our chats over the years about training, mindset, and what it takes to win will forever be imprinted in my mind.

My trainer Kelsey Andries has boundless energy and enthusiasm and has never stopped believing in me. On days when I couldn't get going in the gym, I could always count on Kelsey to bring the energy to kick my ass, rain or shine.

My skills coach Darryl Belfry taught me so much about the game of hockey. He always seemed to know what I needed to do to get better. He helped me change my game, to become less physical and a better playmaker—more spider, less bull, as Darryl memorably termed it. He challenged me to think outside the box and reimagine the game and my place in it. His passion, enthusiasm for teaching, and love of development are contagious, and I will be forever grateful to him.

I couldn't pull off WickFest every year (or this book) without the help of my dear friend Ceilidh Price, the festival director. Ceilidh has been managing communications for me for a decade and a half. If anyone knows how to handle my bad moods, it's Ceilidh! She and her husband, Robb, have become family to me and second parents to Noah.

Dan Kuzmarov has been my agent for 22 years. He has always believed in me and what I do, and I'm proud of what we have achieved in our two decades together.

Through medical school, I relied on five mentors, all of them women. For eight years, Dr. Mardelle Gamble let me shadow her in the ER. She calls me her "black cloud," because whenever I'm around, bad stuff seems to happen. I will forever be grateful for the wisdom, knowledge, and laughs she has shared with me.

I spent the last decade of my hockey career peppering Dr. Wanda Millard, then the chief physician for Team Canada, with questions in the training room. In those years, she became a great friend, advisor, and voice of reason for me.

Dr. Susan Bannister was a key advocate for me through medical school and a great sounding board for any issues I had. She is a fantastic pediatrician who cares deeply for her patients and a true leader in medicine.

I met Dr. Nancy Scholz first as a teammate at the Oval for a season, then again when she was analyzing results of Team Canada's fitness tests and doing all our body fat testing. She was affectionately known as "the fat lady." From the start, I thought she was brilliant and urged her to go to medical school. A few years later, I followed her there! I relied on her strength and wisdom as I navigated the hell that was med school.

Without Dr. Alex Frolkis, an internal medicine resident, I might never have made it through and graduated. Alex could always sense when the pressure was getting to be too much and knew just what to say or do to ease the stress. She is exceptionally brilliant, and U of C GI is lucky to have her!

I spent over 20 years training or going to school at the University of Calgary. Sincere thanks to the top-notch faculty and staff I have worked with in the Faculty of Kinesiology and Cumming School of Medicine. A special and very sincere thank-you to McMaster University for its support as well.

It is an honour and a pleasure to work for the Toronto Maple Leafs, the most inspiring and professional environment I have ever worked in.

It would be unfair to single out any of my wonderful teammates here. I wish I could thank each and every one of you—for the wins, the losses, the ups and downs, and all the crazy, wonderful memories. I am eternally grateful.

This book wouldn't have come to be without a team of people: first and foremost, Nancy Macdonald. Nancy patiently and determinedly painted my ideas and stories into cohesive prose. Ceilidh filled in all the gaps where I had forgotten a key element or perspective. My endlessly supportive editor, Alanna McMullen, was essential in helping me knit together my random thoughts and stories into something whole. I could not have got this book past the finish line without Alanna. The Penguin Random House Canada design, production, marketing, and publicity teams took brilliant care of bringing the book to readers far and wide.

Finally, to my nieces, Bryn and Addy: may you always have the courage to go after whatever you dream of and know that a little girl can do anything a little boy can do. The road I took is a little more travelled now.

Over the boards. Over and out.

HAYLEY WICKENHEISER is regarded as one of the best female hockey players in the world. She has represented Canada at numerous World Championships and made six Olympic appearances (both summer and winter), bringing home four Olympic gold medals. Off the ice, she has picked up numerous additional accomplishments, such as Olympic and Hockey Hall of Fame inductee, accomplished public speaker, Founder of world-renowned Canadian Tire WickFest, and she is currently the Senior Director of Player Development for the Toronto Maple Leafs and a medical doctor.